D1545537

PROTESTANT BOY

ALSO BY GEOFFREY BEATTIE

PROTESTANT BOY

Geoffrey Beattie

Granta Books

London

Granta Publications, 2/3 Hanover Yard, Noel Road, London N1 8BE

First published in Great Britain by Granta Books 2004

'Whatever You Say Say Nothing' by Seamus Heaney from *New Selected Poems 1966–1987* published by Faber & Faber Ltd 1990, reprinted by kind permission.
'Wound' by Michael Longley from *The Penguin Book of Poetry from Britain and Ireland since 1945* edited by Simon Armitage and Robert Crawford published by Viking 1998, reprinted by kind permission of the Peters Fraser & Dunlop Group Limited.

A CIP catalogue record for this book is available from the British Library.

1 3 5 7 9 10 8 6 4 2

ISBN 1 86207 563 8

Typeset in Sabon by M Rules
Printed and bound in Great Britain by
William Clowes Ltd, Beccles and London

Dedication

I dedicate this book to all Ulster men and Ulster women, both Protestant and Catholic, but especially to my father, mother and brother.

Northern reticence, the tight gag of place
And times: yes, yes. Of the 'wee six' I sing
Where to be saved you only must save face
And whatever you say, you say nothing.

Smoke-signals are loud-mouthed compared with us:
Manoeuvrings to find out name and school,
Subtle discrimination by addresses
With hardly an exception to the rule.

Seamus Heaney: *New Selected Poems 1966–1987*

PART I

PROTESTANT BOY

1

I was going home to Belfast to visit my mother. It was the spring of 1998 and the weather was very good for that time of year. My mother lived on her own in Ligoniel, North Belfast, in the little Protestant enclave where I had grown up. Ligoniel is a mill village that once had a mixed population of both Protestants and Catholics, but with more Protestants geographically towards the bottom and more Catholics towards the top.

We call our neighbourhood the 'turn-of-the-road'. It seems a vague sort of term, like saying that you live at the bus stop on the hill or by the corrugated fence on the way to town, but people in Belfast usually know exactly where you mean, which often surprises me. On television, however, they call this area 'Murder Triangle'. It's a Protestant area with murals on the gable walls in tribute to the local men killed or imprisoned for life while in the service of the paramilitary Protestant organization, the Ulster Volunteer Force, the UVF, who re-formed in 1966 on the fiftieth anniversary of the Battle of the Somme, where so many members of the original UVF lost their lives.

The Somme is a key psychological landmark for the

Protestant people of Northern Ireland. In the words of Winston Churchill: 'This was the greatest loss and slaughter sustained in a single day in the whole history of the British army.' That 'loss and slaughter' is one of the main influences on the mindset of the people of Ulster. 'Not a single man turned back' was what I heard when I was a child. 'Not a single one.' A German general – possibly Ludendorff – is reported to have said that the ordinary British soldiers of the First World War were lions led by donkeys, and that the donkeys were the British generals. I heard that saying when I was a child a hundred times.

The area where I hail from is bounded by Ardoyne on one side and Ligoniel on the other, two strong Republican areas, no-go zones for people like me – Protestants, I mean. It is a bleak sort of place; that is the only word that I have to describe it. I had left many years before to go to university and had stayed away. 'You always said that you would come back when you got your degree but I knew you wouldn't,' my mother would say. 'I knew that you were lying to me.'

Going home for a visit was a last-minute decision, a spur-of-the-moment kind of thing. I had rung my mother to tell her the good news.

'Where are you ringing from?' she asked.

'Work,' I replied.

'Can't you afford to ring from home?' she responded. But she sounded excited on the phone, even though she was trying hard not to show it. 'Hire a wee car at the airport and we'll visit your father's grave. Nobody has taken me up there for over eight months.'

I felt guilty already: guilty that I didn't go home more frequently, guilty that she had nobody else to take her to my father's grave, guilty that the grave was not looked after properly.

I arrived at the turn-of-the-road late in the evening in a little blue Corsa, which I had dutifully hired at the airport. I parked outside my mother's front door opposite the library, which resembled a concrete bunker with its wire grilles and the sectarian graffiti daubed on its walls. Some curtains moved next door as I let myself in; there didn't seem to be anybody behind them, just a wizened little hand gripping the frayed edge – probably some other elderly woman who didn't have much mental stimulation. My mother's front door wasn't locked; it was an old habit in a mill village, where everybody had once known everybody else, where there had once been a sense of community.

'Hey,' I shouted into the back room. 'It's me.'

There was no answer. The silence was always telling.

'It's the UDA,' I shouted in a thick Belfast accent. 'It's Mad Dog Adair here. Come out with your fucking hands up.'

Perhaps understandably, there was more silence and no comment, not even on my swearing.

'It's Geoffrey, your wee son,' I said trying a different approach, but still there was no reply. I cleared my throat to break the uncomfortable stillness and went into the back room. There she sat, with her bad legs up on the blue vinyl chairs in front of the black and white television. She hardly bothered to glance my way.

'It's about time,' my mother said. 'Are you sure you can *spare* the time?' she added sarcastically.

I cleared my throat again and pulled out a chair that felt a little greasy. I sat down and stared at the television just to avoid seeing her expression. She usually didn't bother to mask her displeasure, just her happier moods at other times. We sat there for a few minutes. There had been no kiss, no hug. Nor a smile.

I asked her if she fancied a drink.

'I hope that you've brought your own because the off-licence is shut,' she replied. 'You know rightly what time it closes. I've nothing in the house.'

I knew this was untrue – the whiskey was kept hidden behind her make-up bag in the cupboard – but I didn't want an argument.

'Have you any coffee, then?' I asked helpfully and glanced over at her with a slight, friendly smile.

'You know I don't drink that stuff, so why are you bothering to ask?' my mother said, without reciprocating my smile. 'Do you think that I can just nip down to the shops with these bad ankles of mine? No, there's no coffee, there's just tea, but you don't drink tea. Although when you were a boy there didn't seem to be anything wrong with tea. It was good enough for you once upon a time.'

This was the dig I had been waiting for. I had moved away from here, consciously and deliberately, almost culpably, and 'hardly bothered my arse coming back', as she put it. I wasn't interested in my home any longer, she said, or in my own mother: I was too busy enjoying myself across the water.

'You've turned into one of those English snobs now, you've forgotten all about your home and where you came from. "Have you any coffee?"' She imitated my accent, but it didn't sound like me. 'What's the matter with tea? It was all right for your father and me.' She was crying now without turning her face away from the television. 'I'm pleased that your father isn't alive to see what sort of a man you've become. He would be ashamed of you.'

'I only asked if you had any coffee,' I said, trying to defend myself without attacking her. I understood that she lived a drab, monotonous existence. She had never been intended for a life like this.

6

'I was always told that I was the best-looking girl in Ligoniel,' she used to tell my brother Bill and me when we were children, but she had been widowed in her forties. My mother was never meant to be alone, with her bad, swollen ankles, crimson and gangrenous-looking, which meant that she couldn't walk anywhere and had to go up the stairs on her hands and knees like a helpless child. I was all that she had left, and in her anger she liked to remind me that I hardly counted.

'You're no good for anything. You only look out for number one. You've forgotten about me and your family and where you come from.'

The television programme was about an orphanage in Kosovo; I could tell that she wasn't interested in the thin shaven-headed boys and girls. She said that she was going to bed early. 'There's no point in staying up.' I wasn't mentioned; it was as if she was talking to herself. I sat there, wondering why I had bothered to visit her. My brother used to say that only I could talk her out of her soot-black moods. But sometimes I didn't like to bother, that was what I told myself. It was better than admitting defeat in the face of it.

We sat in silence as she prepared to go up the stairs. I mentioned my dog to her, I don't know why exactly. I told her how he had got some premature grey hairs on his face. I thought that she might be amused to hear of a boxer with a grey beard. She wasn't or didn't seem to be.

'You love that bloody dog more than you love me' was her reply.

I was tempted to say, 'Is it any wonder? He never sulks.' But I didn't. I just sat there, thinking of the work piling up at the university in my absence. My mother sighed loudly.

And then, out of the blue, something changed. I don't

7

know why: perhaps even she realized that the sulk was pointless, that it was leading nowhere.

'Go and get me a drink, then – you know where it stays.' She looked over at me. 'And put something else on the TV. Those poor children have no chance in this world, not like the spoilt ones you get over here.'

I got up and went straight to the cupboard.

'You can be the barman,' she said. 'But just remember, don't put too much bloody water in my drink. I like whiskey with a dash of water in it, not the other way round.'

The whiskey looked as if it had been watered down to make the bottle look fuller than it really was. She kept her feet up on the stool in front of her. And each time she said, 'How much water have you put in this drink?' I replied, 'Not much' – quite truthfully, because it had already been watered. And she said that I seemed to like giving her glasses of water to drink.

'You are no drinker,' she often said. 'You're not a proper Belfast man.'

And I just laughed.

2

We eventually talked until the small hours. My mother liked the two of us to talk like that, on our own.

'You only have one mother,' she would say. 'You can have a lot of women, but only one mother. Just remember that.'

As I slowly sipped the whiskey from the glass that had a greasy thumb mark on the side I reflected on the fact that she was wrong in her accusations about me: I have never forgotten where I come from. My family and my working-class background have made me who I am and, in addition, I have always felt myself to be an Ulsterman, a Protestant Ulsterman. But this, I must say, is a private, slightly vague feeling rather than a conscious and clear sense of identity.

Perhaps I was secretly angry at my mother because she seemed unable or unwilling to tell me enough about our own family background and about my Protestant heritage so that I could understand this identity a little better. I have always wanted a clearer sense of who I am and where I belong. After all, the Troubles had been all about identity and belonging. The Catholics of Northern Ireland seemed to know who they were and what they wanted, even if their evocation of traditional Irish culture did seem hopelessly contrived at times. But we Protestants were the other side of the coin. We just wanted the status quo, we wanted to stay British, and she had called me an English snob, where both 'English' and 'snob' were an integral part of the insult.

'I would never want to be English,' my mother always said. 'Or Scottish, for that matter.'

She occasionally told me stories about my family background, about how we were descended from a famous and wealthy family, but I was always left wanting more.

'I'm not educated like you. Why don't you go and find out?' she said.

I told her that one day I probably would.

'You couldn't stop chasing women long enough to have the time,' she said. In her mind that was what I did all day; she believed that the university occupied only a small part of my life. Perhaps this was just projection on the part of the best-looking girl in Ligoniel. Or perhaps she understood her son better than most.

'We're very alike,' she said when we got on better.

It's all in the name, anyway – that's what they say. That was what Seamus Heaney was writing about in his famous poem. My name says it all, you don't need the school. I love hearing of anyone with the same name, love to think that there may be some connection no matter how vague: Trevor Beattie, the advertiser, James Beattie, the footballer, Admiral Beatty – anyone, no matter how tenuous the link. It's a Protestant name, part of that great Plantation of Ulster in the seventeenth century. My family probably came from the Lowlands of Scotland originally, so my name marks me out as a settler, an interloper, someone who does not really belong in Ireland, or perhaps anywhere else for that matter.

I had a friend from Dublin when I was at Cambridge University. On our first day there we met our tutor, an intelligent and cultured man, who asked us to share a room in the psychology department.

'I'll put the two Irishmen together,' he said as he ushered us into a chalk-dusty room. It was probably just small talk on his part, something to say to fill the silence. He left us alone for a few minutes to unpack our boxes of books.

My new colleague looked at me. 'I hate it when people think in crude categories like that,' he said in his Dublin brogue. 'And he's meant to be a psychologist.' He hastily picked the desk with the window to the side and plopped a box of books down on top of the desk, making the chalk dust rise before I even had a chance to look around and get my bearings.

I joined the Dublin man over by the window at his newly claimed desk; I noticed the trees outside already starting to shed their leaves, golden in the sunlight.

'What a great view,' he said with some pleasure.

I had been too slow. I smiled to myself: I knew that I would only have a white wall to look at for the next three years.

The Dubliner looked pleased with himself; his lips curled in a self-satisfied sort of way. 'Two Irishmen, indeed,' he chuckled. 'And you're not even Irish.'

I made no acknowledgement; there was no sound except that of brown cardboard boxes being ripped open to expose paperback books with dog-eared corners.

'Perhaps you should point this out to our tutor,' he continued. 'You're just a wee Protestant from the North, one of the "no surrender" brigade.' And we both laughed politely, embarrassed.

Later that week John – that was the Dubliner's name –

and I were laughing again, in that same kind of way. 'You don't even think like an Irishman,' he said. 'How could anyone mistake you for the genuine article?'

I was thinking of John the other day. A clear image came into my head and I could hear the resonance of his voice. He was always very serious, always discussing profound topics in the field of the philosophy of language – the views of Wittgenstein, Chomsky and Searle – with no hint of uncertainty in his tone. I found it all slightly intimidating.

A number of years after we had left university I learned that he had drowned while on holiday. He had got tangled up in a pedalo while trying to save his son who couldn't swim. Or perhaps it was John himself who couldn't swim. It seemed like a terribly heroic and yet pointless death. We could never have seen anything like that coming, that golden autumn day in Cambridge.

But my memory of John is always tainted by his words about Irishness to me on the day we met.

At Cambridge in the 1970s, the intellectual elite seemed to have a very narrow interpretation of the Ulster conflict. There were just good guys and bad guys: there were the native Irish, 'driven out of their lands', and then there were the Protestant settlers. The Native Americans were fashionable at the time, so too were the aborigines of Australia, and the Catholic Irish seemed to fall into a similar category in some people's minds. Then there were the problems of civil rights and gerrymandering and discrimination, and Bob Dylan singing about times a'changing and Joan Baez reminding all radicals that we, or they – yes, they – would overcome difficulty and walk across that great emotional bridge to Martin Luther King and all those downtrodden people everywhere who had a legitimate dream.

Cambridge may have been the bastion of the Establishment – I saw the Prime Minister and the Archbishop of Canterbury on separate days popping into college for dinner, Rab Butler was Master of my college, and the Butler Education Act was probably responsible for my being there in the first place – but every tutor who dressed in denim and leather somehow saw himself as being the exception to this rule, a free spirit fighting for what was right, fighting for the dreams of others. I had never heard such radical talk before.

And they all had the same predictable position on the Irish question: they were clearly and explicitly anti-Unionist and anti-Protestant. One of my tutor's colleagues wrote a book on the abuses of psychology in the interrogation of political prisoners in Northern Ireland. 'The Protestants will use any means to maintain their position, to keep control of the Catholic population,' my tutor said. I was mainly silent.

'If you like Great Britain so much, why don't you settle on the mainland?' one fellow student at Trinity College asked me in a manner that suggested that he was actually trying to be helpful rather than provocative. 'And let's give Ireland back to the Irish.'

My native city of Belfast was being bombed into some form of submission and I sat in a Junior Common Room high above Great Court and listened to these educated people telling me to leave my home for good. I was feeling trapped and hemmed in by the good fortune that had got me here, while my friends at home battled on the streets to maintain their position. But in my opinion my Cambridge colleagues didn't know much about what that position actually was.

The Protestant ascendancy, that's what they thought. My new friends at college had learned just enough Irish history to know of the Penal Code of 1695 preventing Catholics from bearing arms, educating their children and owning any horse above five pounds in value. They also knew about the final penal law that entered the statute books in 1728 and deprived Catholics of the vote. The words they used were 'discrimination', 'persecution' and 'deprivation' on the one side and 'privilege', 'elite' and 'the ascendancy' on the other. But I didn't recognize my own experience in what they said. And I detected no understanding on their side of the psychology of these Protestant interlopers.

I left my own personal history vague, intentionally so. I didn't want anybody to feel sorry for me or treat me any differently. They asked me about my school and they filled in the rest themselves. One friend assumed that my father was a judge; I have no idea why – I can only assume that he believed that most Protestants worked in the law or were landowners, and because I didn't shoot or hunt my father's profession must be the law. For years this friend asked me about famous trials and the pressures that 'a person who presided over such trials' might be under. He seemed to assume that my reluctance to talk about it was due to issues of security rather than to the fact that my father, who was dead, had been a motor mechanic. He had been a beautiful, gentle man with broken glasses and oil-stained overalls that were never clean because we didn't have a washing machine. He had worked for the Belfast City Corporation in their Falls Road depot.

I never moved back to Ulster after university. The friend who had suggested that Northern Irish Protestants should move to the mainland got it right when it came to me. My link with my own past was my mother, who was getting older. I always realized that when she was no longer here my contact with times gone by would be much more difficult, much more tenuous. But I knew that one day I would take her up on her suggestion that I should explore my past and my Ulster Protestant culture in more detail.

I have written about Northern Ireland before, in 1992, in *We are the People*, a series of snapshots of the Protestants of Ulster. After it was published my mother didn't speak to me for six months: 'You just take the mickey out of me and your home,' was what she said. She only read a few pages and then fell into a silent rage. I had to write a letter to her – interestingly enough, something that I had never done before – in order to beg her to talk to me again.

Now I was interested in reflecting on my own behaviour and speech, and on the processes and patterns that had shaped me. I was keen to find out more about my family history, I also wanted to explore the small actions that take place away from the rhetoric and hold the real key to the thinking of this much maligned people, the Protestants of Ulster. I was not interested in the bombast of politicians, the clap-trap – quite literally, the tricks and devices to attract applause – the cries of 'No surrender', 'Not an inch' or 'Ulster says no', but the more private behaviour of ordinary people.

This book was necessarily going to be a journey – a journey back home and a journey back through time, through a lifetime and through history. And it was always going to be highly personal; it had to be. It would become even more personal and emotional as time went on, as my tenuous and faltering link with Northern Ireland was threatened by the mortality of those whom I loved, those who were my only link with my own past.

The psychologist in me would say that this exploration is based on a very small, heavily biased sample. But, as my mother always said, you have to start somewhere: best to start with something close to home, something that you know about, something that has not been idealized in your own mind – at least, not yet, anyway – something rough and true, something personal, something like a life as lived.

3

The next morning, I slept in. I had heard my mother calling my name, which had woken me up in the middle of a dream. I woke just long enough to recall the dream: it was about her getting the little black-and-white family photographs out of the cupboard for me to look at. They were small, insignificant pictures and I couldn't make out the details in any of them, so I had put them into a large tubular yellow device that functioned as a slide projector to make them larger. But I pressed the wrong button and they came out of the bright yellow machine cut up into strips and I was scrabbling about trying to catch all the bits as they emerged, with her crying in front of me.

But that had probably been hours ago, although I could not be sure.

The alarm clock was not working so I had no idea what time of the day it was. There was no noise from down below now. My mother was probably sulking again. I reached over for my watch and carelessly knocked it down the back of the flower-patterned blanket box that lay alongside the bed. I tried to find it but couldn't. I swore loudly, and then I had to pause to regain some composure before forcefully pulling my hand back out. It was covered in dust and stringy cobwebs. The home help never bothered with these kinds of places in my mother's house, places that she would have cleaned herself when she had been able to do so. I felt guilty, as well as stupid. I still had no idea what time it was; I felt a little disorientated.

My mother shouted up one more time, and then she started talking about me in the third person as if she were discussing me with somebody else.

'Only just home and he's bloody well swearing again,' she said. 'Let's face it, he only pops over here to tell the time.' She always criticized me for not making my visits longer.

I had not slept well and then in the morning, after being woken up by all that shouting, I had fallen into a deep sleep. The mattress was soft and springy and I could pinch its fatness between my finger and thumb. I had a pain in my spine. The pillows were flat and I had a sore neck. Some time in the night I had got up and fetched a towel from the bathroom and folded it under the pillows to make them more comfortable. But it had not worked: the towel was damp, and this dampness had probably made my neck worse. The cheap bed was part of the experience of going home. I could never sleep properly; I was always tired when I woke up.

The walls were thin and I could hear every sound from outside: the voices, the dogs barking at nothing, the coughs in long extended bursts as if intentional, cars changing gear, buses with their engines roaring in what sounded like permanent first gear. You hear a raised voice – the

18

unpredictable inebriated shout – and you listen for the response, the outcome, some form of closure. It reminded me of being young again, the overheard drunken fight in the street, waiting for a bottle to be smashed and the screams of the women, holding their men back and getting pasted themselves in the process. I wondered how people could sleep in their beds around here.

I listened to each car accelerate in turn as if it wanted to get away from this particular stretch of road, and no doubt every driver did. The road led from a Protestant 'ghetto' to a Catholic 'ghetto' – that was what the newspapers called them – so speed could be important even in times of peace like the present. Old habits die hard, after all. I listened out for the possible sounds of joyriders, young thieves demolishing the gears on their way through. But they all sounded like joyriders to me.

There had been quite a few famous sectarian murders on this nondescript bit of road just outside my mother's house: you might recognize the dry-cleaner's or the video shop or the public house if you saw them, from certain angles at least, from a snatch of television news.

It was a dangerous little stretch of road for other reasons as well. A lorry had ploughed into some houses just a few doors down from my mother's house a few weeks previously. The driver had been killed. He was hailed as a hero because although his brakes had failed coming down the Ligoniel Road he had avoided killing anybody except himself. The houses just down from my mother's were wrecked, but my mother hadn't seen them because she could not get out.

'How bad are they?' she had asked me.

'Bad,' I said.

'A bloody mess?'

'Yeah, a bloody mess', I said echoing her words.

'As bad as a bomb?' she asked.

'Yeah, probably.'

She made a long blowing sound. 'What did we ever do to deserve . . . ?' She left the question unfinished and half-looked heavenwards, as if God himself might finally take notice.

When I was a kid I used to hear people talking about 'the Big Fella', and I would sometimes think that they were talking about my Uncle Terence rather than God.

'He'll have to answer to the Big Fella one day,' some neighbour would say about Old Bobby with the greyhound who had thumped his wife in the eye with a potato, which he had picked up whole and unwashed from the table in the back room, or about Big Stoker Cassidy who had hit Paddy the barman with a stool during last orders because Paddy had said that Stoker always went to the toilet when it was his round.

And I would nod along with the talk, from outside the conversation, remembering my Uncle Terence's temper. Old Bobby's wife had wandered down the street with bits of potato caught in the corner of her blackened eye, demanding that everyone survey the damage. It was almost funny, the way that she was stopping people. My Uncle Terence said that he would have a word with Old Bobby on her behalf and we could hear Bobby clattering about his yard, falling against the swinging door of his toilet, knocking over bottles, swearing but not loud enough to provoke my uncle. And the rest of our family stood in silence, listening, with the back door open until it was all over.

What happened would not be discussed; men like my Uncle Terence settled their business like that in those days, man to man, sleeves rolled up, no talk about it afterwards. My father was too soft, that was what my mother said; my Uncle Terry was the big man in the family, the man to look up to. He was married to my Aunt Agnes, my mother's sister; they lived at the top of the Ligoniel Road, the Catholic end. But for years I saw no special significance in that: I just accepted it. I used to forget that Belfast can be very territorial, and that territory can say a lot about who you are.

One of the neighbours had been in my mother's kitchen when the lorry driver lost control of his vehicle.

'Otherwise,' said my mother, 'let's face it, she would be dead too.' And she glanced over at me.

'Let's face it' was one of her favourite expressions. She used it as an introduction, or as a commentary, or as a challenge – to me usually, as if I might be trying to avoid facing up to something. And she always said 'dead' with a very short vowel sound so that it sounded almost violent.

'Like that lovely-looking lad who was driving the lorry; I saw his picture in the paper.'

She always seemed to categorize every man she ever talked about in terms of his appearance, the way some men do when they talk about women, as if it was always relevant to the story. She used expressions like 'not bad-looking' or 'a good-looking fella' or even 'a real film star', which was the highest praise and could apply to both men and women, but mostly to men. And then at the opposite end of the scale there were scathing judgments like 'you wouldn't look at him twice' or 'just ordinary', which was short and to the point. Worse was 'he's an old frigging boke', where boke was onomatopoeic, with a long 'oooo' sound as if retching.

So this driver, and a good-looking fella as well, which made it twice the tragedy, had ploughed into a row of houses just a couple of doors down from my mother. The little stretch of terraced dwellings looked as if they were in the process of being demolished.

You could imagine some visitor from America pausing outside the houses in the street where my mother lived to take in the full extent of the physical and spiritual rebuilding that would be necessary in Belfast. The stranger would survey the guts of the buildings spilt out, gouged, pock-marked, concrete blocks hanging from metal rods, rusty joists holding up what was left of the bedrooms. Heaps of glass, brick and concrete were all ground up together in a grey powder in what was left of a tiny garden.

But no visitor would think of the old dears, the neighbours who had survived this disaster on their doorstep, sitting with their free newspapers, a résumé of the past week's news, spread out in front of them with the picture of the lorry-driving hero on their table, discussing how good-looking he was.

There was no duvet on the bed in which I slept, just a few thin blankets, one made of nylon like something from the early 1960s. True, duvets *had* started to catch on in Belfast but not everywhere, not yet.

I had visited one of my old mates in prison several years previously. Jim was a member of the UVF who was serving eight life sentences for his part in six sectarian murders and two attempted murders. He had been given a further twenty years for a series of thirteen bombings, and possession of explosives, guns and ammunition. He had made the bombs that were used in a number of terrorist attacks: one was a car bomb that exploded at an IRA funeral in the Ardoyne, killing two people; another was a bomb packed with industrial nuts, which killed two men in the Avenue Bar in Union Street in 1976. He had joined the UVF about the time I had left Belfast, when the IRA were trying to blow the guts out of the city; he was going to defend Ulster, to save our Protestant heritage. He said that he was 'fighting a war against the IRA'. But he killed civilians.

I read about Jim on the front page of an English newspaper when he was sentenced. When I went to see him he had just been out for a visit home after fourteen years inside. He told me that when he went into his old bedroom for the first time he thought that his mother had put curtains around the bed because he had never seen a duvet and a valance before. 'They hadn't been invented when I went away,' he said.

That was not all that had changed for him in that time. 'I couldn't get used to money on the outside. I got this taxi one day and the fare was one pound sixty. I was fiddling with these notes, and I could see this taxi driver looking at me. He must have thought that he had a real space cadet in the back.' 'Space cadet' was what we used to call anybody who behaved a little oddly by our standards, who didn't conform to the rules on the street corner.

It was eerie hearing this language from a man now in his mid-thirties. Jim saw other familiar things in a new light. 'I thought that Belfast was the most beautiful place on earth. I thought that all the women were beautiful, and I must have been staring at them. The smell of perfume was overwhelming. In prison your senses get starved. It was lovely just to walk up the stairs and feel the carpet under your feet or to stroke a dog. But my home territory looked really run down. You carry this image of your home all the time you're inside and you're shocked when you see the reality of it.'

This was the home territory that he had been defending by joining the UVF in the first place.

I would ring my mother during the years when I was away and she would keep me up to date with what had been happening back home. She would tell me who else from around there had been arrested or who had been gunned down in the street and who had survived. 'Were you a friend of so-and-so?' she would ask. 'Or was it your brother?'

'It was me,' I would answer.

'Oh, yeah, he was a very quiet wee boy but he's just got life. He did more murders than Billy the Kid – that's what I heard, anyway. And do you remember his brother Davy, the good-looking fella? I think that he's a bit older than you. Anyway, they tried to murder him last week when he was coming out of the wee club. The car drove right up beside him and they just opened up.'

It was odd, having these brutal events relayed to you by your mother who now talked about bombs and bullets as part and parcel of her daily life. She had developed some of the vocabulary for reporting the events.

'Do you remember George Walmsley?' she would ask, and you knew what was coming next; it was never going to be a story about success or good fortune, it was always going to be a tale of despair and probably death, that's how it was around there.

'Well,' she began, 'he was gunned down by the IRA as he

left the Orange Hall in Ligoniel. I knew George from when I was a wee girl. He was a lovely, quiet man. He was coming home early because he was worried about his mother's health. She had just lost her husband; I told you about that at the time, but you probably can't remember it, you were probably too busy to listen. They don't know whether George was hit by gunmen from a car or by a sniper.'

'Oh God, I'm sorry to hear it,' I said.

'You're okay, you're out of it,' she replied, sounding angry, peeved at me again. 'That's what we have to live with. Why they picked on George Walmsley is beyond me, except that he was a Protestant. He was such a quiet man.' There was a pause, and then she added. 'The good ones always get taken – auld quiet George, your father, your brother. It's always the bad ones who get away with it.'

I wasn't sure if she was including me in this, and perhaps even herself, I couldn't be sure. But the story about George was a dig at me, I knew that. George cared about his mother; in fact, he cared so much that it cost him his life.

Another time my mother asked me whether I could remember the Youngers from Wolfhill Avenue, 'up near where your Uncle Terence used to live?'

'Vaguely,' I replied.

'Well, they murdered old William Younger in his bed. He was eighty-seven years old. Do you remember his daughter Letitia? The one who was never married, the quiet spinster woman. Well, she was found with a pitchfork stuck right through her neck. She was pinned to the floor with it and then they shot her in the head and in the chest. And she still wasn't dead.'

'Oh goodness,' I said.

25

'She didn't die until she got to the Mater Hospital. It's desperate in this bloody place.'

An invisible enemy was killing my mother's Protestant neighbours. The killers were a sinister and anonymous group. The locals from the mill village of Ligoniel who were Catholic and who had lived there for generations were trustworthy - 'dead on', in her words – but some of the new ones that they'd moved up to Ligoniel in more recent years from elsewhere were not.

'Some of them are a right bad bunch. I've got old neighbours who are Catholic who come to see me week in, week out, and that's what they say about some of these newcomers from Ardoyne or West Belfast.'

It made my mother angry when she heard representatives of Sinn Fein saying that the violence of the IRA, unlike that of the UDA and the UVF, did not have a sectarian element to it.

'What do they call it, then?' she would say. 'It's all sectarian; there's no other word for it. How can Gerry Adams say that it's not sectarian? Why are they targeting people like George Walmsley or Billy Younger? He knows that it's a lie.'

She had lived there all her life, but she knew victims on both sides, and she would store up little incidental details to tell me, little details that captured the reality of the violence around her.

'Did you hear about your man being shot in Clifton Street? He was a Catholic. They'd had a wee party in their house and then they went outside for a snowball fight. He was shot on his way back to his house with all the snow in his hair and on his coat. He was trying to get back up off

26

the ground when his family found him. It must have been awful to watch. It was like if you've ever seen a dog hit by a car, the way that they try to get on their feet again. And you can see in their face that they know that they're dying, that fear, even auld dogs know it, so imagine what it's like for a human being. It's terrible what they do to ordinary people in this town of ours. And imagine being shot dead because you'd gone outside for a wee snowball fight. How terrible is that? If he'd stayed in that night and just watched the snow fall, he'd be alive today.'

It was hard to look at the houses and the streets and the entries around here in the same kind of way, knowing what had gone on.

'You know that pub near the pet shops in Gresham Street where you used to sell your guinea pigs?' my mother said. 'Well, your man just ran in and shouted, "All right, all the Prods get to one side and all the Catholics get to the other." And then he opened up. They killed five men in there, men just out having a quiet wee drink; three of them were Catholic and two of them were Protestant. It was just indiscriminate murder. And,' she added, 'the gunman was a Protestant. We're always shooting our own. Our lot can be just as bad as theirs, and a lot stupider.'

4

Nylon blankets always give me a rash and leave me cold. I had been cold all night. The bedroom was chilly, but I didn't want to complain. 'You've always been a cold crackers,' my mother used to say whenever I did. I didn't know what the phrase meant.

My clothes were piled over the divan and I had two suits hung on top of each other on a single metal hanger on the outside of her wardrobe.

'You've brought too much stuff home with you,' she had said. 'You've too many clothes,' which sounded like a criticism, but wasn't. 'You take after your mother,' she would say. 'I was always a great one for the style.'

When she worked all those years in Ewart's, the linen mill in Ligoniel, everybody, including Mr Ewart himself on his annual visit to the shop floor, would comment on her style, according to my mother. Mr Ewart by all accounts was a dashing-looking man, 'a real film star'. He wore a patch over the eye he had lost in the war.

'He was like Douglas Fairbanks Jnr,' my mother always said. 'Your father was more like David Niven.'

I never remembered my father being particularly like

David Niven – he'd died when I was thirteen – but my memory of him is mostly from old photographs that show him with his thin hair blowing in the wind on the beach.

This was not the house I had grown up in. This was the new Housing Executive place. It was perhaps fifty yards from where the old one had stood. My mother had been born and reared in 15 Legmore Street, as had I. Her father, George Willoughby, had lived there all his life. Before that she had no idea where her family came from. They had always been in Ligoniel as far as she knew. But before the linen industry came to Belfast?

'I've no idea,' she said, 'I wasn't around at the time.'

And what about further back, what about the Plantations and Scotland? She said that she had some second cousins in Scotland, that was all she knew, but their father had moved there from Belfast and 'he had a wee horse and cart business that he drank away'. But what about before that?

'We've always been Irish' was all she ever said. 'We're not Scottish, they're too bloody mean with their money, and we're certainly not English. Who would want to be English? We're just Irish but Protestants, if you know what I mean. We've always been Church of Ireland too.'

My father, Billy, was from the Shankill: there was no ambiguity there – he was from the very heartland of the Protestant people. He had grown up in Upper Charleville Street, and I knew that his father had moved to the Shankill from the Dromore area. My mother talked about Billy taking her down there when they were still courting, and she told me that his father, Sam Beattie, was a local entrepreneur.

'He had skating rinks all over the place,' she would say.

'That's why your da was a champion skater.'

But I had never seen him skating and I had never been to Dromore, although I had seen the signs to this town on my way to Newcastle, where the Mountains of Mourne do indeed sweep gently down to the sea and where we went camping with the Church Lads' Brigade at Easter. Later my friends and I went there on our own, wearing trench coats, that is to say long, military coats that they really might have worn in the trenches, sleeping without tents and drinking cheap Mundies wine and eating cold creamed rice straight out of the tins, in the Easter holidays after that. We would sleep on the shingle beach or in the backs of lorries or in gardens with low hedges. But despite all these trips to Newcastle from Good Friday to Easter Tuesday, I never once made it to Dromore.

Occasionally, I would search for evidence of my family's past in my house. I would look for photographs of a thin man on ice skates, perhaps looking a little like David Niven, or a picture of Dromore Cathedral, or a horse and cart, or a thatched cottage. But there were no remnants of this kind in our house. There were just a few discoloured photos, which were kept in a Weekend Chocolate box, mostly of my brother Bill and myself when we were young. My older brother Bill, who was a very pretty child, often wore what looked like girl's dresses, made by my mother on her sewing machine, and he sat in toy cars built for him by my father at work. There were photos of me and Bill in matching duffel coats and grey knee socks with our mother looking glamorous and beautiful in lipstick and light buckskin gloves, standing in front of Father Christmas, me clutching my present, which has obviously already been ripped open. Photos of me later, with a roundish face and my arm in a sling, holding an albino guinea pig that is trying to stop itself sliding down my school jumper by digging its claws into my chest, photos of me and Bill with our arms around Spot our dog, photos of my Uncle Terence bursting out of his suit (he was always a big man) and my Aunt Agnes. It was as if life had begun for our family in the late 1950s and early 1960s. All the photos were stored in damp cupboards for years, watermarked and discoloured as if our history too was fading.

The truth is that we are the kind of family that does not leave much behind. I don't remember my grandparents and the house we'd all lived in had had to come down. That was how my mother always described it: 'the house had to come down'. It was bulldozed one summer afternoon in the 1980s in the great slum clearance that had finally reached North Belfast. These old mill houses didn't have bathrooms. You washed in the kitchen in a basin with a drip of water from a spitting, boiling geezer, there was an outside toilet and in the bedrooms there were damp walls with the wallpaper hanging off and small rivulets of water running down them.

My mother was the last resident in Legmore Street to go. She had nobody, not even me. 'You're across the water,' she would say. 'You've got your own life; you don't care. That university keeps you busy. What time do you start in the morning?' she would ask.

'No set time,' I would say, 'except when I've got lectures.'

'How many of them do you have, then?'

'Oh, about twenty or twenty-two,' I would say, as casually as possible.

'A week?'

'No, a year, but there are tutorials and seminars . . .'

But she had already stopped listening. 'And you can't

help your mother get out of her old house,' she'd say. And she would look at me in that particular way, as if to say: 'What kind of son have I reared?'

I used to think that part of the problem was that my mother never understood the nature of academic work. She was used to shift work and having to clock on and off. I would be sitting in the front room doing my homework as a child and she would ask me to go to the shops for a pint of milk.

'But I'm working,' I would say.

'No, you are *not* working; you are just bloody sitting there. I've been watching you. You haven't written anything for about ten minutes.'

'But I'm thinking,' I once said. 'I'm doing creative things in my head while I just sit here.'

'Well, do them on the way to the shops instead – we need milk for your breakfast in the morning,' she replied.

So the old house came down one afternoon when I was not there. I was probably busy thinking creative thoughts at the time. I was always ambitious and I sensed that you had to put your ambitions first in order to get anywhere if you are working class. The irony is that I think I picked that up from my mother.

The rest of the houses in the street were all boarded up and crumbling around her. Rats and mice were overrunning the area. She was terrified of them.

'If I see one of them rats I'll die,' she said. 'The mouse was bad enough. Sadie had to come all the way up here to get it for me with a brush.'

She would talk about the move, and the new life that was to be hers, but mostly I thought that she liked to talk about it because she knew that I suffered guilt simply for not being there.

One of the benefits of the Troubles, of course, was that housing in Belfast, neglected for so many decades, had suddenly become a priority in the 1970s and 1980s. Like everyone else, my mother profited from the government's largesse, which had also brought newcomers from further afield to reside in our mill village as they moved from their overcrowded streets.

'It was June,' said my mother, 'and, as you know, I've always loved to sunbathe. I used to sit out in the yard, but I only ever looked up, not down – I was too frightened of what I might see down there, running around. On the Saturday night there was no gas or electricity in the house. The RUC arrived and I was just sitting there crying in the dark. The RUC contacted the Housing Executive for me, and they sent this electrician up and he put all these new light fittings up for me but the lights still wouldn't work.'

Our street and the others around it, all mixed, had been condemned for years, condemned ever since I was a boy. The bad housing and the social deprivation that it represented were identified as one of the causes of the conflict in Northern Ireland. We were the poor Protestants – not even fighting to keep our footing on a supposedly higher rung on the social ladder, just pawns in someone else's game. That's what those with a socialist perspective always claimed: the working class in Northern Ireland was divided on religious grounds, and hence easily conquered.

They had a point, that was what I always thought, but my mother told me that I was just talking bloody nonsense. And it irritated her to hear about the poor Catholics all the time. The Rocks in our street were poor, there were eleven of them in a house the same size as ours – but Joey Donaghy next door wasn't impoverished and the fruit shop at the top of the street and the off-licence at the bottom of Lavens Drive and the pub were all owned by Catholics.

We collected bottle tops from Brady's, the off-licence just down the street. I had hundreds of these bright winking buttons kept in cardboard boxes with low sides, like trays, and I can remember the 'shooooo' sound when I tilted the box up and they slid from one end to the other. Kieran's, the fruit shop, gave me their old lettuce and carrots for my guinea pigs, which overran my yard when I was in my early teens. The Catholic Bradys and the Kierans were kind to us, and they were better off than we were. My mother liked pointing this out and also liked to remind me that they had proper families to help them move. She had nobody.

'The workmen had to help me out,' my mother said. 'It's bad when you have to rely on strangers.' And for years after she moved, when I asked what had happened to my grandfather's little black sequined cap, which he'd brought back from India and that always prickled my head when I put it on, or the jigsaw of the Battle of Waterloo or the pop-up book about weasels or even my dozens of school books or the books that were prizes for attendance at Sunday school or church, their disappearance was always blamed on the flight from the old house.

'The workmen were lovely but they never gave me the time to get out,' she said. 'Everything was bulldozed away. They told me that there wasn't much point in bringing the carpet from my old house or most of my clothes. Everything was damp; everything had mould all over it. I left a lot in the old house, including the sewing machine, which I didn't mean to leave. I had to get out in such a hurry in the end. After over sixty years it was such a last-minute thing. I'd

34

been born in that house, but I never looked back when I left, not once. When I got to the new house, I went straight to the bathroom. I bought a new flannel and a sponge. My friend Sadie bought me a brand new back-scrubber. I had some fancy Yardley soap and talcum powder that your Aunt Agnes had bought me for Christmas a few years ago. I'd been keeping it for the new house. The only problem was that it had been sitting getting damp in the old place. I didn't want to unwrap it until I had got a bathroom of my own. By the time I got the packet open, I realized that the talcum powder was damp right through. But I've still got it sitting out, even if it is a funny greeny-blue colour. It's an expensive make, you see.'

I have just one or two photographs from the 1960s of the old house as a backdrop to our lives: my father bending down feeding the pigeons in the street with a fag hanging out of his mouth; or Tommy, one of our neighbours from that time who still lives near my mother, standing there with a big wave in his hair. The front door was always open. The hall, that cramped space between the front door and the inside door, was where we entertained our friends in winter. One of my mother's jokes was about the refined wee Belfast man invited to a posh house for tea who needs the bathroom. 'Where's your yard, missus?' he asked. 'Where's your yard?' my mother would repeat. 'As if your yard could be upstairs.' You could just about turn in our yard to track the sun. 'A lovely wee suntrap,' my mother liked to say. 'There's no wind out there.'

I missed the old house. I never liked the new one in the same way, and occasionally the old house pops into my dreams in one form or another. But it's never cold or damp in the old house of my dreams: it's always just warm and cosy and the whole family are in there, along with my Uncle Terence and Aunt Agnes, and we are all laughing out loud, laughing at something on the telly in the corner, but I don't know what the programme is. I can't imagine what would make us all laugh like that.

The old house was the only embodiment, such as it was, of our family's cultural history. It was the place where my mother was born and where her mother had died one Saturday morning when my brother Bill had been sent upstairs to wake her and returned to tell us that she was dead. It was the place where her father had talked about his days in the British army in South Africa and in India, the small place with no privacy where we had celebrated my father's life and untimely death and my brother's life and even more untimely death in the Himalayas, the place where my Uncle Terence, the big man in our family, hid his tears twice. The only place that we ever knew as a family that could link us to our past.

And now that had gone.

5

My mother was sitting in the kitchen and the portable black and white TV was on. She was sipping from a glass of pale amber-coloured liquid, which she tried to hide from me. I gave her a few seconds to hide it properly by taking myself off into the front room.

Her main daily contact now was with the district nurse. My mother would rise early and soak her ankles in a basin of water to loosen the bandages. Then a nurse would call. Some my mother liked and some she didn't. Some, she said, were far too rough with her. Most liked to compliment her on her appearance. 'Your mother always kept her looks,' one said to me. 'She's got lovely skin. What kind of moisturizer do you use on it, Eileen? It must be something very expensive.'

'Just soap and water,' my mother replied. 'That's all I need.'

I hated looking at her ankles on her tanned legs. Her legs were usually dark, which made it worse in a way. She'd always had good skin that tanned easily. We were proud of our complexions in our family. We would compare tans all summer long. She swore by coconut oil. At primary school

I was called 'the darkie' or 'Paki' because I spent hours sitting in my yard glistening with coconut oil when the sun, Old McCormick, was out.

Margaret Donaldson said that my tan was fake; no boy could be that brown, she said. Nobody else in our street was that dark. It was the tan of Victor Mature, of West Palm Beach, of Hollywood itself. Not the tan of rainy Belfast. It was a deep mahogany on the back and on the shoulders, lighter on the legs and the thighs. It was worthy of comment in the street: people would talk about us 'looking well' and say things to my mother like 'Oh, I can see that you and your Bill and your Geoffrey have caught the sun.' We wore our sleeves rolled up to show it off.

The oil came in little tins that sat in the cupboard from one summer to the next. It was hard but it turned to liquid in the heat of the sun; you had to be careful not to spill it. We all sat in the couple of square feet in the yard that got the sun for a few hours a day. My mother would say 'Old McCormick's out,' and we would go out to sunbathe. We went for walks in the park but we didn't sunbathe there, nor in the street: the yard was where we sunbathed, in private. And if we were lucky we kept the tan for the rest of the year.

But Belfast can be such a wet, drab city. My visual images of early childhood are all to do with rain, of sitting on the big chair by the window, watching the rain on the wet slates of Barginnis Street, looking down at the shiny wet roof of Heron's, the hardware shop at the bottom of the street. I can still smell the damp coats singeing in front of an electric fire. I can see the greyness of the streets, the puddles in its rough uneven surface, the concrete the colour of mouldy bread, with the sloppy line down the middle.

I remember the day when they laid the concrete in our

street. It was never level, not even at the start. I can remember the smell of the workman's hut at the top of Legmore Street, when they were mixing the concrete. The workman was there to keep an eye on it, and all the gang snuggled into the little hut with him and sat on his wooden bench, next to his coke-burning stove, and he told us dirty jokes and taught us songs about sailors down by the docks in Belfast. He said that he was pleased that he had some good company for a change.

I have images in my mind of the rain pelting down, the door blowing open, and my father coming in through the door after five, his overalls stained with oil and wet with rain, his glasses all steamed up. I can smell the oil on his overalls whenever I choose, mingling with that damp smell of Belfast rain and the sweat of the workman.

I have never in my whole life smelt like that. I have done physical work, certainly: I have worked as a labourer on building sites and I have piled boxes in naval stores and I have even stood in a foot or two of salty water, skinning the gizzards of chickens coming at me upside down on a blood-spattered production line, sometimes alive and twisting and turning, the way that human beings might do, anticipating what was to come. But I have never been a *working man* in that sense.

I could hear the church bells ringing, and although I couldn't remember his name I had a clear, almost perfect image of the old man who used to ring them when I was a child. He was a small man even by the standards of Ligoniel, stooped, his face lined, thin grey hair patted down with spit. In that same black crumpled suit week after week, he was almost funereal-looking. He had a folded-up umbrella nestling in the crook of his arm, dandruff on the collar of his jacket and a white shirt that was probably wrinkled everywhere except the bit that was visible. He had an even stride like an undertaker. His wife had died years before. I can't remember which house was his, except that he was from the turn-of-the-road. I didn't see him on any other day of the week, just on Sundays.

As he made his lonely way to church, we boys used to say hello to him, in a sort of ironic way, almost sneering. He would say hello back, as if he didn't or couldn't recognize the joke.

'Are you coming to church?' he would enquire.

'Oh, yes, of course, we wouldn't miss it for the world,' Colin would reply. Colin, my best friend, was like that, a real funny man, the kind you need on the street corner to keep the craic flowing, although we spelt it 'the crack'. (The other spelling was a bit too Fenian for us.)

My mother called Colin 'forward' or 'a cheeky wee shite', depending on her mood. I was the quieter one; he was the one with all the cheek in him. My father called Colin 'Wee High Heels'. I don't actually remember him saying this, but my mother always said that he did, and she brought this up every time Colin was mentioned. Every time I thought of Colin I thought automatically of his wee high-heeled boots. Cuban heels on a twelve-year-old, a pretty pink face that was always trying to hide his emotions, hide his guilt. We were always hiding something, always covering our tracks. Whatever you say, say nothing, that's what they say around there.

But Colin always did lie with that same compressed smile that grimaced out at you. It was not much of a cover for anything, and he was always singled out for punishment because of it. He smiled in that particular way when he had something to hide and when he was just nervous and even

40

when he was excited but wanted to hide that. He seemed to be smiling at people all the time. He had buck-teeth and was very self-conscious about them – he kept his mouth closed when he wasn't giving cheek. He hated being called 'Bugs Bunny'.

'You wouldn't want to be late, Tommy,' Colin would say to the old bell-ringer in an attempt to make him break that slow deliberate stride of his. And you would see Colin's buck-teeth appearing as his lips parted. But Tommy never hurried and five minutes later, at a quarter past eleven, you would hear the bells ringing, that stately rhythm, and Colin and myself and Michael and Bill would make our way to our pew, second from the back on the side aisle of the church, the far side opposite the side door – on Christ's right arm, so to speak. That part of the church was invisible from our mothers sitting on their own in the nave. It was side-on to the minister in the pulpit who could not see us without deliberately turning our way. But he would sometimes pause in the middle of a sermon to throw disapproving looks at us.

'Was that Colin that the minister was looking at during the sermon?' my mother once asked. 'Were you boys talking again in church? I wouldn't like to think so.'

I looked out of the window and noticed that there was some graffiti on the gable wall of what used to be Bill Gowdy's house. Bill Gowdy was my best friend before Colin came along. Bill represented the innocence of my early childhood, the years before Colin and his cynicism. Bill's initials were BG, mine were GB; he lived in 51 and I lived in 15. There always seemed something deeply significant in this symmetry at the time. However, he was a Presbyterian and I was Church of Ireland and he once told me in the barber's one afternoon after school that the Church of Ireland was closer to Roman Catholicism than Presbyterianism because of all the ornate stained glass everywhere in our churches. 'There's not much between you,' he had said, 'when push comes to shove.'

The new graffiti on the side of Bill's old house was a warning to the residents of the houses further up the road. It read 'Ligoniel Will Burn' and 'Taigs Out'. 'You Have Been Warned,' a final line added. I wondered who had written this stuff. I was sure that I would know them and their families.

When I left Ligoniel for the University of Birmingham I had the strange experience of reading about my friends on the front pages of newspapers. A number had been murdered, some had become notorious killers, many just got by. 'Survive', that was my mother's word. 'You just survive around here, you don't live properly.' Those who had been murdered were sometimes killed by Republican groups, sometimes by their own side.

Bill Reynolds, who had been in the Church Lads' Brigade with me years earlier, was shot dead by the IRA in 1987 at the turn-of-the-road in the Village Pool Hall, where he was the manager. It was half-ten in the morning and Bill was playing pool with a local lad. Some man, not even bothering to wear a hood, walked in and said to Bill, 'All right, mate?' He opened fire with a sub-machine gun and, for good measure, then shot Bill six times with a revolver. The IRA claimed that Bill was a leading member of the UVF but in reality he was a low-ranking member of the UDA, involved in prisoner welfare work. As Jim Watt said to me when I visited him in the Maze: 'It was just because Bill was an easy target, nothing more. You wouldn't have taken him with you on a message, let alone on a job. He worked as a manager in that snooker hall, day in, day out. Just an easy target.'

'Freddie Reynolds snookered' read the graffiti half a mile down the road at Ardoyne; they even got the name wrong. Then an IRA man from the Ardoyne area was shot dead in a social security office. 'Gino signed off at last' read the graffiti at the turn-of-the-road. It was all tit-for-tat, even in the sick attempts at humour.

Another friend, Robert Thompson, 'Tampy', was found dead in an entry in East Belfast in 1975. He had just been released from the Maze. He had been beaten and kicked and then he had had his throat cut and had bled to death. He was twenty-three years old; his killer was a twenty-year-old Protestant.

Dennis Eccles, who was in the UDA, was shot dead in a drinking club in Silverstream. None of the witnesses agreed on exactly what had occurred that night. Some armed and masked men had come in to steal a gun from an off-duty UDR soldier who was having a drink there. There was an exchange of gunfire and when the smoke cleared Dennis was found lying on the ground. It was never clear whether he had been one of the masked men or not. The coroner at his inquest said: 'We have heard a lot about Chicago-type killings in Belfast, but this was more like a Wild West saloon-type killing as portrayed in the pictures. Here we had two outlaws coming in and starting to fire in all directions.'

Jim Watt and other friends always said that they had joined the UVF to fight a war against the IRA. But it was a strange, undisciplined sort of war. Sometimes it really did seem more like the Wild West than any conventional war I could think of.

6

My mother told the same old stories again and again. They were mainly stories about my father, and about my brother and me when we were young. I hadn't known any of my grandparents, and my father had died, so my mother was the one thread that connected me with my own past. Sometimes I would quiz her about her own father, who had been in the army. But she was vague about where he had served. She knew that he had been in India and South Africa, but what about the First World War? Had he been at the Somme?

'I don't know,' she would say. 'For flip's sake, I wasn't born then.'

I just wanted some concrete past, a past that I felt I knew a little about, and a survivor of the Somme for a grandparent would have done this. South Africa and India were too vague for me. Every boy in Belfast knew something about the Somme: the men not turning back, walking to their deaths in the service of the Crown, a true blood sacrifice, perhaps one of the greatest blood sacrifices of all.

The gable walls in the Protestant areas of Belfast were

there to remind us of all of this, 'lest we forget': one mural showed the men of the 36th Ulster Division going over the top – three soldiers with fixed bayonets, seen from the front, running towards the enemy with no fear on their faces. Although the truth is that this particular artist was so bad that he probably couldn't have depicted fear even if he had wanted to. On a gable wall in Donegall Pass there used to be a memorial to those who had died at the Somme. The painting showed the heads, hung in silent prayer, of three darkened soldiers. And the link with the present could be seen in another gable-wall mural in Craven Street commemorating the seventieth anniversary of the Battle of the Somme: on the left a member of the 36th Ulster Division in 1916 in battle dress, and on the right a contemporary member of the UVF clad in black and 'banged up' in Long Kesh prison camp, with barbed wire in the background.

Sometimes it was just easier to let it be, to let my mother talk. She was happiest talking about her husband and her other son. They had both been taken away from her, speedily and without any real goodbyes. My brother died in a climbing accident in the Himalayas when I was twenty-six and he was thirty. My father died thirteen years before my brother when he, my father, went into the Royal for what were supposed to be some routine observations – at least, that was what he told the family. He didn't want to worry us.

My mother and my brother and I visited him the night before his exploratory operation. In my last conversation with him, on the Sunday night in the Royal, I told him that one of my guinea pigs had died, just for a joke. He had looked really concerned and had sat up in bed in his blue striped pyjamas, his glasses falling forward on his face.

'No, I'm only kidding you, da,' I said, laughing. 'I'm only joking.'

And he laughed, relieved for me; those were the last words I ever said to him.

My mother's stories were always introduced in exactly the same way. 'Do you remember . . .?' she would ask when starting one about my father, and I would nod in a non-committal sort of way because the truth was that I didn't really remember many important details about my father but was too ashamed to say so. I think that it was a sort of defensive forgetting, a form of repression to ease the pain. But I had heard the stories many times and my father had been reborn in the telling and I could do nothing about that.

But I have images of my father as well, disconnected images. I remember the way he smiled and the way his glasses sat on the end of his nose when he was reading. I remember how he stretched his arms out to put his coat on and how he tugged his cap down on his forehead. I recall the way that he read the paper, the way that he held it, but funnily enough I don't remember the name of the newspaper that he read. After he died we didn't buy daily papers any more. We were just given papers at the end of the week by a neighbour. The newspapers came in a used and crumpled pile, five at a time, and were kept under the cushions on the settee in the front room.

I can recall vividly the night of my father's death, of course, and my Aunt Agnes being annoyed that nobody had come to pick us up to take us to the hospital to see him. I can see the expression on Agnes's face, and that on the face of my Uncle Terence, the Big Fella, who stopped us going into the hospital after my Aunt Agnes and I had travelled there by bus. I remember the rain that night, the puddles in the car park of the Royal.

I remember my father resting in his coffin in the front room for three days and how well he looked with all that powder on his face, in the glow of the pink lampshade. I remember my cousin Myrna, who had anorexia, coming in on the day of the funeral and everybody stopping and looking at her. We had tea after the burial at Roselawn cemetery in her house, my Uncle Jack and Aunt May's house, because it was bigger than ours and they had a proper wooden dining table, not just a formica top that doubled up as other things. Myrna died a month later and lies in the row next to my father's in Roselawn.

I remember how my father walked and, as I've already mentioned, the smell of his overalls. But his voice had faded in my memory. I watched a TV programme the other night in which a hypnotist said that human memory is a bit like a video recording of life, with all the events stored on some kind of biological spool, waiting to be played over and over again if you just know the right way in. If you just have the key to unlock it.

Yet no matter how hard I tried I only ended up with fragments of images and events. I remember that afternoon up the Hightown with me kicking the rugby ball about, my father lying there reading his paper, his glasses over the end of his nose, the smell of the air. I can remember booting the ball up into the air and chasing it over the ground that was covered in prickly yellow gorse and loose, sharp brick. I remember feeling the rough brick through the soles of my thin trainers and then stumbling on a shard of broken glass, which somehow managed to pierce the side of my ankle. My father had to carry me back to the car. I don't remember how his voice sounded or what we talked about that day. I just remember him struggling under my weight, and wheezing with the effort. I remember that his glasses dropped off on the way back, and that he had to put me down on the wet grass while he picked them up. His glasses fell off a lot: the frames were loose.

I remember these smells from my father. Engine oil that's been on the road and has seeped into old overalls. His nickname was 'Half-shaft' because he worked as a motor mechanic. He worked with bus engines and smelt, even on his days off, of the oil that they put into buses. Old overalls, weeks between washes – we didn't have a washing machine in those days.

For years I liked to pick up oily rags and hold them right up to my nose and breathe deeply, to breathe my father back to life. I was caught doing this once about a year after he died by a woman in our street. She thought I was trying to get high on something and she said that she would tell my mother. 'Run away off home,' she said. 'Run away off home.'

After my father's death, I wanted to keep his clothes as a way back to him. But my mother gave them all away to his brother, Jim. Jim had been drinking the day he came to collect them and he wouldn't come into our house. He waited on the street, too shy or awkward to come in. He just stood there, waiting for an armful of my father's clothes to be carried out to him.

I wanted to keep something of my father's. I scoured the cupboard above the TV and found the case for his glasses in the bottom of a little wicker basket where my mother kept her sewing. The glasses themselves had gone, so I was left with the case. It didn't smell of him, it just smelt of old plastic, and the spring had broken so the case didn't snap shut the way it should have done. But I used to just lie on the bed and look at it, trying to conjure up some missing parts of him. But it didn't work. My memories weren't under voluntary control: some bits came back on their own but most stayed hidden. And many were lost.

I can remember Colin, 'Wee High Heels' himself, in those same boots, shuffling up beside me on the day of the funeral, saying that he was sorry. He had lost his own father a few months before so it meant something. And him telling me afterwards that I never once looked him in the eye on the day of the funeral. I kept my gaze fixed on the ground the whole time. I walked behind the coffin without ever looking up.

I can't remember how my father talked or laughed or cried or shouted or cursed – the sounds, I mean, the tone and timbre of his voice. But I can see a woman with long tangled hair, that old alcoholic from Lavens Drive whom we used to torment, Minnie something, getting into our house the night before the funeral and trying to kiss him in the coffin. I can even recall the way she did this, like a film slowed down. I saw it coming, I could read her intentions. Nobody else seemed to realize what she was doing there. 'It's terrible what drink can do to you,' they were all saying, but I knew that Minnie liked my father. She was saying that my father was a good man, too good for round here. And then I can visualize her leaning over the coffin. I remember somebody shouting that she shouldn't be allowed to slobber all over him like that. That was the word they used, 'slobber'. I can remember how she sounded as Big Terry tried to pull her away and get her out the door.

There was some sort of scuffle. My mother was crying

and my brother Bill and I looked at each other. I remember the sound of Minnie sobbing on the street outside, the big door being slammed, Minnie banging the door to be let back in, and then her crying getting fainter as she made her way home. And everybody in the room paused to listen: all the talk and all the crying stopped for a few moments.

A few silent moments.

It was Big Terry who had to intervene with Minnie. He was the man about the house; my father was far too soft – that was what they all said, the same old expression. Terry lived at the top of Ligoniel and he taught me how to fish with my hands in the streams above Ligoniel on warm summer nights, standing on wet, slippery stones, tickling the bellies of the trout.

The top of the Ligoniel Road was the more Catholic part, although for years I didn't put two and two together and work out that Terry might have been a Catholic. It was inconceivable. He would pay me sixpence to sing the Sash right into his face, and my father and mother would laugh. I never saw the joke, but a joke it must have been. 'THE SASH MY FATHER WORE.' I would sing it so close to him that I would be spitting right in his face. 'IT WAS WORN AT DERRY, AUGHRIM, ENNISKILLEN, AND THE BOYNE'. And my uncle would let out a big cheer after each place name as if he personally had been at each of these locations and had fought on the right side in each conflict – the winning side, the Protestant side.

One day, many years later, one of my Catholic friends told me that he had seen my Uncle Terence going into chapel. It was Kevin Rock, and he said it with a note of triumph in his voice. When the Rocks came to my birthday party they had to bring their own cups because there were so many of them, but at least I invited them. Their house smelt and if I had to wait there after school for my mother to come home from work I would hold my nose for hours on end.

We had the first car in the street and the first TV, and the Rocks would line up outside the front window to watch. My brother Bill would pull the curtains and laugh, but my father would give them spins around the streets in the car.

It was Kevin who told me that my Uncle Terence was a Taig – his word, not mine. A big fucking Taig just like him, the exact words fresh in my memory. The man who taught me to box, to tuck my head in right behind my fists, to fish with my hands, to stand up for myself on the street, that man was a Fenian bastard. All Kevin's own words. I was ashen-faced all that day and night. It was as if one certainty in my life had been overturned. Then I noticed the St Christopher in his car and was worried that my friends from the corner might see it. They might even see him going into chapel.

Terence bought my suit for my confirmation in St Mark's church. 'There are not many who would do that for you,' my mother had said at the time, and now I knew what she meant. She meant that there were not many Roman Catholics who would do that for a Protestant boy who was being confirmed as a Christian.

My Uncle Terence lived in Lesley Street and some Saturdays I would take my box of cornflakes folded over at the top, and my pyjamas, and go up Ligoniel to sleep between my aunt and my uncle in a house that smelt different from ours. That was how close I was to them.

In the morning they would sometimes let me go and play on the dump at the end of the street. When I reach back in this conscious and deliberate way, I can feel a slight nausea when I think of the dump, not because of some of the terrible things that undoubtedly happened there during the Troubles but because of one night in summer when I was eleven years old, when I disappointed my father. I can remember so little about him, really, but when I start to conjure up Lesley Street in my mind I can smell the dump and see his face for a second, and I can't get either the smell or his expression out of my mind.

It was all to do with my fort, which my father had made at work. He told me that he was going to bring something home for me and I waited for him for an hour at the bus stop at the top of the street. It wasn't my birthday; it was just a present that he had made for me in his spare time at work. I saw him in his oil-stained overalls and with his glasses on, getting off the bus with something large wrapped in newspaper. He was a slight man and he could hardly carry it, but he was smiling, because he knew that I would be very pleased when I saw it. He tottered as he held it in front of him. He wouldn't open the present until we got into the front room at home. The dog was jumping all over the furniture, sniffing the paper and barking excitedly, tearing at it with his sharp teeth.

I had never seen anything like it before. It had brown metal ramparts with zigzag steps shaped out of a single piece of aluminium and it stood on a hardboard base. The whole thing was solid and well put together. It must have taken months to make in my father's spare time at work: every bit of metal had been shaped by hand. I had received an expensive Christmas present that year – a Cape Canaveral-type rocket base with missiles that fired. But the fort was different. In these rows of identical mill houses all crouching in that hollow below the hills that ring Belfast, street after street of them as far as the eye could see, all with their cheap identical flowery settees bought on credit from the same shops at the bottom of the Shankill, and the same pictures on the wall of foxes, fawns, infants, in fact anything with big eyes professing innocence and adoration, there was something individual and unique about the fort, made in and for love.

And made for me.

I had hundreds of toy figures in a large rusty circular tin that stayed in the damp back room – cowboys and Indians, Confederates and Yankees, knights called 'Swap-its' whose legs and arms moved and could be swapped over, Russian soldiers with red stars on the fronts of their grey winter hats. The knights on horseback were so intricate and such a delight to look at that my mother put them on display with all the best items in the china cabinet. Two knights, the Red Rose of the House of Lancaster and the White Rose of the House of York, were on parade on the top shelf. We weren't allowed to go near the china cabinet or feed the gas meter, which was just behind it. And when you wanted to play with the knights you had to ask for the key and remove them with a very steady hand from the glass-fronted cabinet, which always seemed to tremble and shake with all that china inside it.

I can still remember the smell of the china cabinet. All the smells that I have experienced in this life – the lavender in the quiet fields beyond Sainte Maxime, the close-up smell of drying seaweed on those wild gull-squawking shores north of Santa Barbara, the fragrant smell of leather in the market in Hammamet with mint tea in the background – I can still smell the inside of that cabinet with greater ease and with greater clarity than any of them, as if I have just leaned into it and breathed again. Don't ask me to describe the smell; it must have been some kind of cleaning material that had evaporated inside over many years.

All the toy figures eventually found their way into the fort. It was a generic sort of structure though it looked like Fort Laramie, from the Wild West as depicted on the black and white television. But my mother told me that her daddy had been to a fort like that in India. George Willoughby, she called her daddy, just in case I thought it was George Bell, who was my cousin. My father knew of George's days in India and this might have given him the idea that guided his craftsmanship. British soldiers of the Raj patrolled that fort at night in the corner of our front room, but no shops seemed to sell models of the enemy, whoever the enemy were. But that didn't matter to me, a boy with a fertile and vivid imagination, living in a damp, crumbling mill-village house, who could spend hours on the floor just playing.

But one Thursday in July when I was eleven we were going to my Uncle Terence's and my mother told me that I was now too old for the fort and the soldiers. She was tired of cleaning my knees with Vim because of the amount of time that I spent on the floor.

'You're too old to be on your hands and knees all the time. Too old for that sort of childish nonsense.'

It was all done in a matter-of-fact sort of way, as if it was no big deal. The fort got in the way in such a small house. We kept it in the back room, where the wallpaper hung in great moist swathes from the slimy green wall with the damp running down. The fort was going rusty like the metal container that held the figures, like the tools we kept there, like everything else in the house. It had to go and it was loaded into our car, I don't know who by, perhaps my brother. I was told that the poor children up Ligoniel would love it. I was told that I had had my enjoyment. It was somebody else's turn. I was assured that the children up Ligoniel weren't as well off as we were. They had no model missile sites, or garages with lifts that could be wound up, or forts made at work by their fathers in good jobs. I knew that these children were from big families, families sometimes with no work, Roman Catholic families. 'Too bloody idle,' our neighbours liked to say when Big Terry wasn't around. But I didn't really understand why they only said it when he wasn't there.

There was a steep hill at the end of Lesley Street; we just called it 'the dump'. It wasn't an official refuse site, it was just where people dumped all the stuff that they didn't want. I remember old settees with rusty springs sticking out and black bags full of open tin cans with large black crows picking at the bags and hardly bothering to move when you approached them. My mother told me to leave the fort out on the dump. She told me that it would be found, and that one of the boys from Ligoniel would have a childhood filled with imagination because of that fort, the fort that my grandfather had fought in and that my father had made by hand.

My uncle came with me as I laid the fort out in the middle of a hill of refuse. Dust and hairs, human and dog, filled all the cracks in the hardwood base, the hairs ingrained and dense like thread. But it was well looked after. That's another expression my family liked. The fort, the car and the front step that my mother would wash every couple of days on her hands and knees. A white froth on the pavement outside the house would be swept away by basins of cold water. All well looked after, all cared for. Loved, if you like. It was a very Protestant way of thinking about these things.

So I carried the fort and left it in the middle of this long slope filled with human debris. A beautiful handcrafted object that had been at the centre of my childhood – indeed, still was at the centre of my childhood. That, perhaps, was the problem. My mother had decided that at eleven I shouldn't be scuttling around the front room on all fours with cowboys and Indians and Russians.

We all sat in my uncle's front room, my Aunt Agnes, my father, my mother and Terence's mother. There was a crucifix on the wall as you came in. I had only ever seen one in the Rocks' house. I never understood what it was doing in my Uncle Terence's home before Kevin Rock explained. My mother always said that it was something to do with Terence's mother. I didn't know what, though.

But I couldn't stop thinking about the fort. I was always told that I was spoiled compared to some of the boys in my street, and especially compared to the boys at the top of the Ligoniel Road. I always thought that meant Catholic boys with their big families and their crammed houses, the same size as ours but packed with five or six of them to a bed, where they would sleep top-to-tail. They would run into their own house in the afternoon to dip dry bread in the sugar bowl that stayed in the cabinet in the front room, or they and I would nick a few spuds from the back of the potato lorry to roast in an open fire up the fields, and they would beg food.

'You are spoiled rotten,' my mother would say in our back room that had water running down the walls. 'And don't forget that.'

I knew that I had more toys than any of them but still I didn't want to give the fort away.

I don't know where I got the hammer from; it must have been from the toolbox in the back room of my uncle's house. It was a big heavy claw hammer. I hid it up inside my coat and said that I was going out. The fort was still there, just as I had left it, in the middle of the dump. No deprived child had got there yet. I sat down on the slope beside it.

I suppose that it was almost like playing again. The first blow flattened two or three of the metal ramparts. The second removed one section of the metal steps. I sat on the dirty stones among the piles of rubbish and hammered away. I wasn't emotional about what I was doing. It was a cold act. I was just determined that no child, no matter how deprived or how needy or how hungry, would get my fort where my grandfather had fought for the British Empire, where Davy Crockett – whose father came from County Londonderry – had held out against the Mexicans at the Alamo, where my dreams of lands far away from cold damp mill-village houses that turned everything to rust had been nurtured.

I was obviously engrossed in my little frenzy of destruction because what I remember next is my father and uncle standing over me. My father looked almost puzzled, perhaps a little hurt that he had a son who could be like this. I looked up at them. I felt ashamed and embarrassed. I needed to explain my actions, to justify myself. I remember what I said quite clearly. 'It's dangerous,' I said. I remember those very words just coming out. 'Those sharp metal ends, they could hurt somebody. You can't just leave it here. Somebody might cut himself on it. I was just making it safe for them.'

I was led away by my father and my uncle, who didn't say anything at first or even look at each other.

'Let's just leave it the way it is,' said my father eventually.

'But it's ruined now,' I said. 'It's ruined.' I was crying by now, sniffing loudly, wiping my nose on my sleeve. I remember looking down at the trail of smeared snatter along my sleeve – there was just so much snatter. It was a whining, imploring sort of crying that accompanied my excuses. But why I was crying I don't really know: perhaps it was being caught red-handed, the guilt of the whole thing, the fact that there was no way to hide my shame. Or perhaps it was just my way of showing them that I was still a child who needed to dream, whose time had not come to leave these particular things behind.

I can remember the look on my father's face to this day. It would be nice if I could conjure up a more positive look after all these years of trying, perhaps a look of pride in me, but the look that night on the dump is the one that I am left with, no matter how hard I try to change it.

That's the point about human memory: we are not in control of its content nor of its retrieval; rather, it seems to enjoy controlling *us*.

7

My father was proud of my academic achievements, even so. I was 'good' at primary school. Indeed, I'd always felt a little different from my friends, ever since I'd started at St Mark's Primary School. At first I thought that it was just something to do with my memory or even my neatness: neat handwriting on the walls of the class and a funny sort of memory. I would memorize any sort of list that was presented to me – short books of birds and their habits, short books of historical facts, short books of famous authors. I would get my father to turn to a particular page in my *Ladybird Book of British Birds and Their Nests*, and I would recite whatever fascinating information was on that page about the brambling or the whitethroat or the red-backed shrike or the stonechat. Birds that I would almost certainly never see and birds that I wasn't really interested in. And I could count very quickly, faster than anyone I've ever met since.

'I'm a good counter as well,' my mother always said. 'You take after your mother.'

She ran the Christmas club in the mill where the women put money away each week for Christmas presents for their children. They trusted my mother with numbers that would add up correctly and with the cash, which was perhaps more important. The house was full of scraps of paper and cigarette packets turned inside out with pounds, shillings and pence totalled up in soft black eyebrow pencil. She had been the teacher's pet in her class, chosen to sit at the front, and then a generation later it was my turn. Mr Welshman, the headmaster, remembered my mother: 'a very pretty and clever girl, who could have been something if she had been born somewhere else.'

I thought the same might be true of myself, and that this was his coded way of telling me.

But then, when I was eleven, this world, my world fell apart. I passed the eleven-plus. It was a Saturday morning, and the thick brown envelope came through the letter box.

'Is it thick or thin?' Bill shouted down the stairs – from bed.

'Thick,' I shouted back, fumbling to open it.

'Oh shite, he's passed.'

My brother, you see, hadn't. We were no longer in the same boat. I had been pushed out and now I had to swim away to strange and foreign shores.

I had chosen the poshest-sounding school on the list that the local education authority had sent out – Belfast Royal Academy. There were a few other schools with 'Royal' in the name as well but this one sounded the poshest of them all. I didn't know where it was. But then, I didn't know where any of them were. After I passed the exam, and not before, the school asked to have a look at me, probably quite sensibly because nobody had passed the eleven-plus from St Mark's Primary School in Ligoniel in living memory.

The eleven-plus turned me into a kind of local celebrity: people would stop me in the street and press sixpences into my hand. It wasn't that Ligoniel necessarily produced children of below average intelligence who were incapable of passing this particular examination; it was just that there was no special preparation for the eleven-plus at St Mark's. While other schools were running special courses on how to perform in this test, St Mark's just didn't bother. One morning they simply informed us that the eleven-plus was to take place the next day. Albert Cowley thought it was a medical examination – 'to see if you're well developed enough to go to Everton Secondary School'. Albert didn't even bring a pencil next morning, but he was wearing clean underpants. I had six new pencils and two new rubbers. I wasn't taking any chances.

Some of the boys from St Mark's went on to university eventually, but they all had to go to the local secondary school first. Albert never made it very far in the end, and he became a binman – although, as my mother says, if you're not frightened of a bit of dirt it's a very good job – 'good pay, short hours, and plenty of little perks'. Anyway, I was being given my big chance – a chance of an education, with a job almost certain to follow where the perks wouldn't depend on what you could scavenge from bins. But first I had to get through the interview.

My mother took the day off from the mill to go with me. My father gave us directions to what he always insisted on calling the Royal Academy School. I wasn't sure if it was the same place as Belfast Royal Academy or a completely different institution. 'Don't let me down,' my mother whispered as we got off the bus.

The driver could see that I was apprehensive. He knew my father since he worked at the Falls Road depot. 'Show them what you're made of, sonny,' the driver said as I got off. I thought this was the last thing that I wanted to show them. On this more than any other day, I knew that I could not afford to be myself.

The headmaster of Belfast Royal Academy interviewed me personally, and apparently this was quite significant. I'm not sure that he knew where Ligoniel was, even though he did look very learned. He wore a gown. He asked a few simple questions and I provided a few simple and truthful answers. Until, that was, he asked me about the last novel I'd read.

My heart sank. There were novels in my house – invariably obtained as prizes from St Mark's Church or Sunday School for excellent attendance, but they were just that: prizes. I didn't really read them. I did take encyclopedias to bed with me every night – the *Everyday Encyclopedia, The Encyclopedia for the Younger Generation, The Living World of Science, The Wonder World of Nature*. I wasn't really interested in fiction but I did have a book about famous authors. Luckily I'd been to the King George V Memorial Hall the previous Saturday to see the film *Gulliver's Travels*. From my *Encyclopedia of Famous Authors* I knew that the original story had been written by Swift, J. (1667–1745). The only problem was that my friends and I had been thrown out shortly after the interval for throwing marbles at each other. We always took bags of marbles to the cinema – it was part of the night out. The only exception was when we later went to see the midnight movie at the Park Cinema on the Oldpark Road, where we'd take old rags to first soak in water and then throw, during the horror movies. But that day in the interview, it was *Gulliver's Travels* or nothing. I was short on plot – I had missed a lot of it, after all, because of the excitement with the marbles – so I concentrated on visual description. I got to the point where I'd been thrown out and said, 'Would you like me to continue?' The headmaster said he'd heard enough. He was already impressed by my ability to conjure up complex images and scenes from the written word.

I was in.

It was a brave new world that I was entering and it scared the life out of me. I took two buses to get to the school; all the friends from my street could walk to theirs. I went to the official school outfitter to be kitted out – white shirt, grey flannels, cap, rugby shirt, cricket flannels. A cap! I have always felt there is a lot to be said for school uniform. On the surface at BRA, or 'Great BRA' as we sang in the school song, we all looked very much the same. Below the surface, though, everything was different. I could never understand how anyone could be so unworldly as to write a school song praising a great bra. I used to snigger at the words, and my school friends told me not to be such a 'pleb'. I didn't know what a 'pleb' was.

'Plebeian, Beattie,' they would explain, 'you're just a plebeian.' I, fortunately, was none the wiser.

But Great BRA did broaden my horizons: I met children who had been to America for their holidays, I met a girl who had been to Saudi Arabia! I'd never even been across the water, as they say in Ireland. And when I opened my mouth, my accent was as thick as buttermilk. But it wasn't just my accent, it was my whole style of speaking. I was surprised to hear eleven-year-olds say, 'He's such a sarcastic and ostentatious person.' I used to look the words up at night in my *Little Oxford Dictionary*, and practise them the next day. 'Don't be be so sarcastic, E. J. Henshaw,' I'd say.

'Why, Beattie?'

'Because I'll stick my toe up your arse, that's why,' I'd say.

My linguistic habits were deeply ingrained – my accent, my vocabulary, my whole style of speaking – even at eleven. One marked feature of the Belfast dialect is the regular occurrence of the expression 'you know'. At times it almost seems to act as a universal punctuation mark: 'I have to get the bus here in the morning, you know, sir, that's why I'm a bit late, you know. Sorry, sir, it won't happen again, you know.'

Pupils and staff alike tormented me. One day, during a history lesson and in front of the whole class, the deputy headmaster decided to rid me of this irritating nasty little working-class linguistic habit.

'I know that I know, Beattie. Would you kindly stop saying "you know"? It's you who doesn't know what you're talking about.'

The more he insisted, the more I kept saying it. He told me to get a grip on myself, and I tried, you know, I really tried.

I learned to hate the sound of my own voice.

I could never be part of the BRA crowd as long as I continued to speak like that. There was no hiding it. I just had to open my mouth and there it would be – out of its cage, circling the room, with everyone staring up at it. I would be asked to give an oral account of Gladstone's contribution to British politics, and even the stupidest and least imaginative boy in the class would snigger at my attempt because of how I spoke. I worried about this blemish the way some boys developed a worry, bordering on the pathological, about their acne. They thought that when other people were looking at them they were always staring at their bad skin. I always assumed that when people were listening to me they were concentrating on my poor speech.

The boys with acne ended up not going out; I ended up not speaking.

When we had to write essays at school about what we did on our holidays, and the other pupils wrote adventurous – and true – stories about meeting members of the Saudi Royal Family *in Saudi Arabia*, I wrote about hitch-hiking to a seaside resort about sixty miles from Belfast. This was a real adventure, as it turned out – my mate and I were picked up by a man, coincidentally a retired teacher, or that was what he said, with a quite exceptional interest in what we had down our trousers. He told me that he could tell that I had a hard-on. When I said that I hadn't, he asked me to prove it. He kept suggesting to us that we should stop to relieve ourselves.

My mate asked, 'Do you mean take a piss?'

We assured the man that we didn't need a piss or any other kind of relief. But to children grown accustomed to tales of Saudi Arabia, trips to Portrush – even when they involved lifts from strange men – were hardly big news, and I was too ashamed to write about what had really happened anyway. The account, as I described it, was not very interesting.

The other pupils asked me if descriptions of trips to Portrush were really the best that I could do.

'I never had the chances you had,' my mother said to me. 'In my day, the only chance you had was no chance.'

I spent the next seven years of my life dividing my time between life on the corner and a life of Mathematics and

Russian and History and Physics. Sometimes it was hard to keep my two worlds apart. My memories are of those moments of intense friction when the worlds almost collided. A friend from school, 'Hamster' was his nickname, arrived at my house one Wednesday night to get some help with his school work. Raymond and Tampy were there talking to my mother, and somebody dropped a lit cigarette into Hamster's pocket that reduced his school blazer to a burnt fragment of cloth.

His father stood in my front room an hour later with this small burned rag, demanding to know who had done this. But my mother defended my friends and said that whatever had happened had not happened in her house because she had been there the whole time. Tampy and Raymond were trying to stop themselves laughing; you could see it in their faces, and I was amazed that nobody apart from me noticed. My mother thought that Tampy and Raymond were both very polite and well-behaved.

On another evening Tampy arrived when I was in the house alone, doing some Maths homework, and asked me to get into a stolen car, which he drove badly over the hill past the police and the army. We were not stopped despite his erratic driving: if we had been, I know that my life would have turned out differently. It was only when I got out of the car that I realized that he was wearing leather gloves so as not to leave fingerprints all over the vehicle's interior and I wasn't. He hadn't thought to warn me.

On another occasion, our gang went to a party in a house on the Shore Road. There was a fight and the house was wrecked, and we stumbled back along the Shore Road pursued by a gang wielding broken bottles. I stumbled and somebody tried to jab a broken bottle into my face but I stopped it with my left hand and the bottle was dropped and shattered. And later that night a friend from school, Hackers I think he was called, and his father found me lying on the pavement somewhere near the Antrim Road. They took me back to their house and plucked glass out of my neck with tweezers and bandaged the middle finger of my left hand, which bears a slight diagonal scar to this day.

What did my school friends think of this other life of mine? I never asked them. I always assumed that there was a sort of spurious glamour associated with my real mates and their fights.

But for me it was about survival. We were getting into a lot of fights whenever we went out. The Catholics and the middle-class boys from school might have liked Bob Dylan or Joan Baez. We liked Marvin Gaye – 'I heard it through the grapevine'. We loved the soul music in the clubs, but we ended up being barred from all the clubs in town for fighting. Every time we went somewhere it wasn't really a question of whether there would be a fight but just of when it would happen – and with me there was always a degree of nervous anticipation – so that we constantly had to be ready with our moves. And then the next day everybody would stand around and talk about who had done what, and what moves every person had used.

'Did you see Bill's cousin on top of the table getting the boot in to your man with the harelip?' somebody would say.

The talk seemed to be a way of working those fast, fleeting images of fury and swearing and violence that just provoked confusion and dread in me – and, I suspect, in many of the others – into some sort of coherent account that could be retold and relived in a meaningful fashion.

'We were ambushed that night. It was a set-up. Did you see your man on the corner, he was the lookout, he must have signalled to the rest of them lying in wait.'

And so it went on. Films from the Forum or the Crumlin or the Stadium picture house gave us the basic structure for many of our stories.

Somebody brought a hammer to a disco and hit some thin fair-haired Catholic lad on the side of the head with it. This was turned into a funny story. 'Did you see his eyes after he got the dig on the head? It was like something out of a cartoon.' I can remember the eyes even now, opening wide, the pupils dilating, a stunned expression. Tampy said that he would knock some total stranger down with one punch at the same disco. So he selected somebody in the corner, some lad who had gone to a lot of trouble to dress up that particular night, and Tampy cracked him on the chin and the boy went down with Tampy on top.

'What did I tell you?' he said when he returned to our little group. But then there was a dispute as to whether the boy would have gone down if Tampy hadn't fallen on top of him.

All my friends knew that my mother never cleaned my bedroom because I had every inch of the walls and ceiling covered with posters of Paul Rogers and Rory Gallagher and pictures from *NME* and cobwebs cascaded down around them. So friends occasionally asked me to look after stolen gear for them. The gear ended up behind my wardrobe or in my chest of drawers, just waiting to be reclaimed.

One night Tampy arrived with some small heavy object wrapped in an oily rag. He asked me to hide the item. I asked him what it was but he said that I didn't need to know. We stood in my hall arguing about this, until he unwrapped a small handgun. He said that he had got it off a relative and he was worried that his mother might find it. I told him that I couldn't look after the gun for him because my mother had started cleaning my room.

'You're a fucking liar,' he said.

But I was adamant.

'Show me,' he said.

So when my mother went to the toilet outside we nipped up the stairs. I can still see Tampy's face as he stared in disbelief at the cobwebs and the dust.

'She cleans in here?' he asked. 'Are you sure about that?'

I swore on the Bible that she did but I admitted that she might have missed a few spots here and there.

'Your mother needs fucking glasses,' Tampy said as we came back down the stairs.

'What were you boys doing up there?' asked my mother.

'Oh, nothing, Mrs Beattie,' said Tampy. 'Geoffrey was just showing me his lovely room.' And Tampy went away that night with the gun.

When I went off to the University of Birmingham, Tampy and I lost touch. The lads in the gang were never great letter-writers, and neither was I. When I came back in the vacation I heard that Tampy had been arrested and had got three years for some offence or other. Soon after his release he was beaten and stabbed to death in a brawl with some Protestant – he was killed by one of his own.

To this day, I had always believed that Tampy's prison sentence was for theft. But having recently read David McKittrick's *Lost Lives* I have now discovered that his stretch was for possession of a gun and that he'd been arrested not long after the time that I convinced him that I couldn't look after a particular weapon for him. I didn't realize at the time how close a call it really was.

We got into skirmishes with gangs from other areas, usually Catholic ones, but sometimes we would pick on the nice Protestant boys in our own neighbourhood. We called them 'The Perfume Gang', but they weren't even a gang, just a collection of lads from the Boys' Brigade hanging around outside the Mayfair sweetshop after a night of drill and gym. Once we had labelled them a gang we thought that it was legitimate to pick on them, for sport. The violence wasn't driven by sectarianism as such. The targets were simply stooges in our dramatic performance as hard men. They were just young men whom we didn't know that well and therefore didn't have to care about. They say that the conflict in Northern Ireland is all about group conflict, 'them' against 'us', but then it was more about 'us' than about 'them'. It was about solidarity and being in a group and looking good when the action started.

Or at least not looking bad.

Some of my mates went tooled up after a while. It was safer, and in some ways easier. Other gangs were tooled up, so some of our gang had to be too. I couldn't have used a knife or a bottle or a hatchet, but one night I was loaned a chain because I was going to a disco far away from our home territory. I borrowed the chain off one of my mates from the corner. I had no intention of using it; it was just meant to make me feel safe. But that night some drunk, swaggering middle-class rugby-playing youth, whom I vaguely recognized from school, punched me for very little reason except that I got in his way. So I picked myself up from the floor and hit him twice on the head with the chain, once with a forward swing and once with a backward one as his legs buckled under him before he hit the deck.

I could have been expelled over this incident but I wasn't caught, although everybody knew that I was the assailant. As the lights went on in the disco, some unknown hand reached out and took the chain away from me, just before I was searched. If I had been expelled and my academic future had been taken away from me just then, as the Troubles were deepening, I know that I too would have been in one of those cars that went out looking for trouble. I couldn't have avoided it.

This was my only real act of violence, and what was interesting was that my mate who had loaned me the chain said that he deeply regretted it. He never let me borrow it again. My mates were always looking out for me, one way or another.

Like a lot of my friends, I had nobody at home except my mother to discipline me or even to give me advice. My Uncle Terence and Aunt Agnes had left Belfast soon after my father's death. Terence had worked at Sydenham in the Royal Naval stores but said that his promotion was always blocked because of his religion. They moved to Chippenham in Wiltshire. My brother served his time as an apprentice electrician at Scott's where he was presented with a Bible when he joined the firm. He finished his training and then went off to climb mountains in the Alps or Afghanistan. My mother always said that he should have stuck with his trade.

If I wanted help I went to the gang. Once there was a fight at my girlfriend's house when some gatecrashers tried to get into a party, so I got my mates from the corner to help me sort it out. If anybody tried to bully me, I would tell Tampy or Raymond, and they would come and sort them out. That was the way that it was and I am sure that was the way it remained when the Troubles got worse, and the gangs from this street or that street became parts of the UDA or the UVF – still fighting for their own little group, still looking after their own.

I was trying to balance this world with life in a grammar school, studying during the day and after I had finished my homework going down to the corner for a bit. I really did feel like the odd one out. But sometimes, my mother said, me being different made sense.

'We haven't always been poor,' she would say to Bill and me. 'I heard that from my great-aunt. Have you heard of Dunville whisky?' she asked. We would be sitting in front of the fire in our pyjamas. 'Have you heard of Dunville Park? It's up near the Royal; well, we're descended from the Dunvilles. We are Dunvilles, in fact. That's probably where Geoffrey gets his brains from – from the Dunvilles. You want to see the house that they've got. It's all white and they used to have horses and carriages. My mother told me all about them.'

'Are you sure about all this, ma?' asked my brother. 'Why are we living here, then?'

'Because we are,' she would say.

'How do you know all this?' he asked.

'Because,' she continued, 'my great-aunt used to tell me about seeing Lady Ann Dunville come to visit her in a coach and horses when she was a little girl. Your great-great-grandfather was a gamekeeper for the Dunvilles and he got one of the girls of the house into trouble. And that's where we come from.'

My brother started laughing. 'We're descended from Lord and Lady Dunville, then?'

The dog came into the room. He was wet with the rain, and he smelt bad.

'I can smell that he's been rolling in it again,' said my mother. 'I've never seen a dog like it. He shites and then he rolls in it. Don't be stroking him, Geoffrey, until it dries off.'

The dog nudged its way towards the fire. We sat there.

'We're from old money, so to speak. We're from a very good family. Ask your Aunt Agnes, she'll tell you. Or your Uncle Terence. He wouldn't lie. Ask him about the Dunvilles.'

I heard the story about the Dunvilles many times. I have even told it myself on occasion, when I have been asked how come a professor like myself comes from North Belfast. 'It could be true,' I say. 'You never know with these things.' And I watch the faces of those I am talking to, and I am sure that I can discern a small change in how they look at me: I'm no longer the boy from the ghetto, but somebody with much better blood altogether.

PART II

STORIES AND SILENCE

8

I told my mother that it was time for my run. She just shrugged her shoulders. She was past arguing with me; running is my daily ritual. Wherever I am, I run. There are no excuses for not going. I have been doing it since I was about thirteen years old. I have run marathons and half-marathons but they do not compare to that daily grind, which does not even permit a day off after a marathon. I have run across dog-infested hills in Tunisia, I have run along a motorway in Sweden in the middle of the night in a snowstorm without a clue as to which direction led back to the centre of Gothenburg, I have run along the Pacific Coast Highway in California, just off the plane and suffering from jet lag, with no pavement for protection and with wide gaudy red and yellow trucks almost brushing my legs.

The fact that my father died of heart-related problems when he was fifty-one may have something to do with all this, but running itself is a dangerous activity. I have always thought that I will probably end up dying while crossing some busy road in the driving rain with my eyes half closed in that state I get into which causes people, cars and lorries going past to become an unimportant blur. I never warm up. I just put the gear on.

'I'm off,' I shouted in to my mother who was confined to her kitchen.

I ran down to the turn-of-the-road, just fifty yards or so, and then around the corner towards the Horseshoe Road. There were two elderly men wearing cloth caps at the corner. They had been at that very same spot the last time I'd been home. They both nodded at me as I approached.

'Running again, eh, Geoffrey?' one said.

I didn't know his name, but I recognized him and I was pleased that he recognized me.

'Still training away after all these years?' he added.

I just smiled back.

'You'll be doing the Olympics if you keep on like this,' he shouted after me.

'The Paralympics,' his friend shouted. 'He'll be crippled after all that training.' And they both laughed.

There were two thin, shaven-headed boys on the pavement in front of me, going back home with milk and bread. They heard my steps on the pavement and spun around.

'One, two, one, two, keep it up,' one of them shouted as I ran towards them. He set his carrier bag down and mimicked the act of running as I passed, running on the spot, running that takes you nowhere. 'Keep it up, keep it up,' he bawled at me, and then he started running beside me, pumping his arms furiously, as if that somehow mimicked my movements.

I was looking towards the Cave Hill, focusing on my route, trying to pick out a path on that distant elevation that we call a mountain, a path that I would soon be following away from these grey, depressing, pock-marked shops at the corner. I always remembered the turn-of-the-road as a place vibrant with life and vitality, not this dead grey area populated by old people with shopping bags and discount drink and men who didn't leave the house in the afternoon.

'Who can blame them?' my mother would say. 'If you'd been through what they'd been through, you'd want to stay in too. There has been a lot of suffering around here.' That was true enough: some of the lads that I had grown up with hadn't had a proper job for the last fifteen years.

You might recognize that corner. Roy Suiters in the greengrocer's was shot dead by the IRA in front of his sixteen-year-old daughter, both pubs were burned down by the locals, and then one was rebuilt and someone was murdered in it. Even the Chinese who ran the local takeaway were lined up and shot. This was rumoured to be a punishment shooting, but punishment for what nobody was totally sure, except my mother: 'They were dealing in drugs. The UDA can't stand for that, not right under their noses.' A Republican paramilitary group murdered Andrew Johnson, the sixteen-year-old lad who worked in the video shop, and the man held to be responsible, Conor Maguire, who lived at the top of the Ligoniel Road, was murdered by a Protestant paramilitary group. Then Maguire's funeral cortège was stoned at the turn-of-the-road by an angry mob.

I saw all this unfolding on television in England over many months, with English friends tutting and commenting on the barbarity of life 'over there'. I met an RUC officer in a nightclub in Sheffield and he asked me where I was from. When I told him he said, 'Oh, you come from Murder Triangle,' as if it was the name of a street or a small picturesque square.

I just nodded. 'I suppose I do,' I said.

That small part of North Belfast has seen over six hundred sectarian murders in the past thirty years. That's getting on for twenty per cent of all those killed during the conflict. Murder Triangle, an area locked into tit-for-tat sectarian killing, almost tribal in its senselessness – that was what the news seemed to imply. Many of the survivors bore the emotional and psychological scars, but there were very few psychologists who ever made it up this way to talk to them or to attempt to understand their experiences.

Those who had survived sectarian murder attempts often had 'flashbulb' memories of what had happened – detailed, almost sensory recollections with all the sights and smells and tastes captured in some permanent mental store. Psychologists have suggested that such life-threatening experiences are recorded by the brain in a quite different way to all other memories. The brain registers everything, just in case this information might be relevant to survival in the future. But, of course, we still have to make sense of these images and sensory experiences in some sort of narrative structure when we attempt to recall what occurred.

Everywhere I went in Belfast I heard people, ordinary people, trying to come to terms with what had happened to them, or, in some cases, with what they themselves had done. The psychologist in me wanted to listen more carefully and to analyse the accounts, and perhaps even to help the individuals concerned. My mother said that there was little that I or anybody else could do. They just had to come to terms with what had happened to them in their own way, she said.

The Cambridge psychologist Sir Frederic Bartlett had called this process of translating fragments of memory into stories 'effort after meaning'. We have to make sense of our images.

But any account from memory is a complex process: the narrator has to decide at some level what to include and what to leave out, where to start the story and where to end it. They have to build images of themselves and of the others in the story, they have to provide some context to aid others' understanding and, perhaps as importantly, to aid their own. It's obvious that history is constructed, but so too is human memory when we move from the personal images and thoughts that we keep in our heads to the words that we need to express them.

Marion owned the local video shop, the shop where the sixteen-year-old boy was subsequently murdered. One night a masked Republican terrorist tried to murder her. He drove right in front of her, blocking her in, and he tried to shoot her in the face but his gun jammed several times. That was the only reason that she was still alive.

On one of my visits home, Marion told me the story. We were in her video shop, which she was trying to sell – she didn't feel safe there any more, not surprisingly.

'One of the taxi drivers had just come out of the side street, and I waved to him and it was what do you call him? It's Big something, I can't think of his name now, but he's got one of those distinctive orange-coloured Hyundai Stellars. So, as I say, I waved to him, and then I got into my car, and the next thing was I'd turned the car on and I looked out and I saw the colour of the car coming up and I thought it was him pulling up beside me to speak. And I was actually going to push the window down, you know, to speak to him, but then I noticed that the car just came and drove right in front of me and blocked me in and I thought to myself, 'What's that stupid bugger doing?' But then the next thing was I looked and, at first, I couldn't believe that it was a gunman standing right in front of me, and you know the way that you sort of think, 'God, I'm seeing things here,' and then he pointed the gun and fired but nothing happened. He had a mask and all on him. All you could see were the two eyes. When I first seen him get out of the car I thought automatically that I was taxiing and that he was going to hijack my car, and I thought, 'Ah, Jesus, they're going to take my car on me.' But then, as I say, when I seen him click like that and nothing happened, I thought, 'God, he's going to shoot me,' and then it just suddenly dawned on me that this was an attempted murder sort of thing. So, as I say, he cocked the weapon back and tried again and in the meantime, I'm sitting there frozen to the spot, I couldn't find first gear, I couldn't find reverse gear. Panic stations. And he pulled the thing again, he pointed again, clicked again, but it still wouldn't go. This was the third time that he tried and then the fourth time he started hammering the thing. So I sat back and I thought, 'God, is he going to hit me in the face, or is he going to hit me in the chest?' And I just sat back waiting and I just pictured the window smashing in all around me. All I could think was, 'God, is this going to feel sore? What's the pain going to be like?' And then he tried hammering the thing again and I thought, 'Right,' and I looked over at my brother David just outside the shop. You could see poor old David struggling to get his car into gear and he was blasting the horn on the van, trying to draw attention to what was going on but then the gunman realized that nothing was happening with the gun and then he just hopped in his car and he was off.'

You can hear the detail in Marion's memory – her brain has

done its job and recorded every detail for all time, to haunt her while awake and asleep. And then the experience has been structured for the telling. Marion is locked into a narrative laden with intense emotional meaning. And as a story, of course, it is perfectly coherent and it all makes sense. It is a story of a heartless Republican terrorist trying repeatedly to execute in cold blood a passive female victim who is frozen with fear. A passive and innocent victim, indeed so innocent that she could not even interpret the signs of what was about to happen to her until it was far too late. A victim who thinks that when people drive in front of you in Murder Triangle they are coming up to you to say 'hello'. That is how innocent Marion was. Language does not simply reflect the world out there; it is used actively to construct it. You can see how an event like this, as described, *demands* some form of retaliation.

We often underestimate the power of language to affect our thinking. Every time I heard about the violent incidents that occurred in my home area, I thought about this. Alex Greer was a Protestant who lived in the same street as my Uncle Terence in Ligoniel. He was shot dead early in the Troubles at the junction of Mill Road and Ligoniel Road, just standing at the street corner gossiping with a friend of his who was sixty-seven. That's what men often do in the evenings around there; they go out to the street corner for a chat rather than being stuck in the house in front of the television. The killers were aged seventeen and fourteen at the time of the shooting. One of the accused said in court that he had heard that two Orangemen were to be shot. That was one sort of label for Alex Greer, I suppose; 'a local', 'a harmless local', 'an innocent man', 'a Ligoniel man born and reared' are just some of the other possibilities.

Language here, even the mere label, starts to direct our thinking before the event, and after the event it provides a partial justification for the action. 'We got an Orangeman today' sounds better somehow than 'We got old Alex Greer, our old neighbour of years and years.'

Danny O'Connor, on the other hand, was a Catholic from West Belfast, shot by the UVF outside his home on the Springfield Road in 1987 as he was unloading last-minute shopping before a family holiday in Spain. His wife heard him cry, 'Oh God, oh no,' before he was killed. The UVF claimed that he was in the IRA and said that: 'Of late he had been used in surveillance work in the Shankill Road area, being spotted on several occasions in places frequented by Loyalists.' Surveillance work is one possible description of what this man may have been doing on the Shankill. There are many other ways of describing his visits to the area.

Why did the violence perpetuate itself for so long in this area? Why did the communities not see the senselessness of such tit-for-tat killings? Presumably because atrocities of the kind Marion described against such innocent victims as herself need to be avenged, atrocities in which her innocence cannot be in any doubt because her misinterpretations of the attempt to murder her are an integral part of her memory of the event.

But how could you describe paramilitary violence against unarmed individuals in ways different to Marion's account? How could language be used to change the apparent significance of what has occurred? Reading Loyalist paramilitary publications like *Combat*, where official statements from the UVF are reported, you can see how:

'On Sunday 14th June at 8.30 a.m., an Active Service Unit

of the Ulster Volunteer Force, in a commandeered car and armed with high-powered handguns, attempted to force their way into the home of IRA activist Cormick Caughey in Atlantic Avenue. The Unit breached two security doors but were unable to break down a third and were forced to abandon their mission. Whilst leaving the area one of the Volunteers fired a warning shot at a civilian who attempted to impede the withdrawal of the car.' (*Combat*, July 1992)

'On 4th March 1992, a four-man Active Service Unit of the North Armagh Brigade, Ulster Volunteer Force, armed with assault rifles, ambushed a vehicle on the outskirts of Portadown, shooting dead the driver, James Gray.' (*Combat*, April 1992)

'On Sunday night, the 13th December 1992, an Active Service Unit of the Ulster Volunteer Force, with the full authority of the Combined Loyalist Military Commands, mounted an RPG-7 rocket attack on a canteen in Crumlin Road Prison.' (*Combat*, January 1993)

This is how it can be done. We Protestants, even when we attack a lone individual in his own home, do so professionally. The emphasis is on the hardware (the high-powered guns, assault rifles, RPG-7 rockets) and on the military intelligence and careful organization underpinning the attack (against IRA activists and a canteen used by IRA men). A vocabulary of military words and metaphors is employed, constantly harking back to the First World War and the Battle of the Somme, with articles introduced with 'Lest We Forget' and signing off with 'Age Shall Not Weary Them' or 'And In The Morning We Shall Remember Them.'

According to *Combat*, Republican violence directed at Protestants is fundamentally different from Loyalist activity targeted against Catholics:

'Pearse Jordan was in the IRA. Pearse Jordan was shot running away. How often have we seen and heard of members of this evil organization running away. They ran from La Mon, Teebane, Claudy, Coleraine and Coleraine again, Lurgan, Enniskillen, and on, and on, and on.' (*Combat*, January 1993)

'They prove their "bravery" time and time again by their selection of targets in their own homes and carry out their attacks regardless of sex or age of the occupants. Recently one squad shot blindly through the windows of the house of a Protestant in the Shankill area, wounding the man and his young grandson. The blinds were drawn in the home at the time and there is no way the would-be murderers could have known who was there, and they fired indiscriminately into the room.' (*Combat*, February 1993)

Loyalists are portrayed as engaged on missions based on military intelligence; they fire only 'warning shots' at civilians rather than actually shooting them. According to *Combat*, Republicans, on the other hand, shoot through blinds without a clue as to who is really behind them. The emphasis is on the disciplined and 'military' nature of Loyalist fighters and the anarchic and flawed style of Republican terrorists (cowardly, opportunistic, indiscriminate).

Marion was married to a member of the security forces and

may have been seen by some Republicans at the time as a legitimate target – or perhaps it was a case of mistaken identity, and they were actually looking for her husband. The Republican gunman who tried to kill her could have been viewed as on a dangerous mission, having slipped through the Loyalist defences. It could, from an alternative viewpoint, have been a story about cunning terrorists – even shrewd freedom fighters – carrying out a dangerous mission behind enemy lines, working undercover at the bottom of the Ligoniel Road rather than at the top.

I thought about all of this as I headed up the Horseshoe Road on that very stretch of tribal territory mentioned in the story, where some of the sickest things had happened over the past two or three decades.

'How's it goin'?' a man of about my age in a cheap leather jacket said to me as I passed. He was out walking a small stumpy wire-haired terrier that looked up at me almost with embarrassment as it scrunched its body up to shit.

'Not bad, mate,' I replied in a chummy sort of way as I ran past him, acknowledging one of my own with that special tone which I use when I'm home.

I got to the Horseshoe Road bend and I noticed all the litter swept by the wind into the bushes, clinging there as if people here were past caring about these things. There were a couple of scraggy ponies in a field opposite the one with the railings. I turned up towards the right on that old familiar road, the Hightown, which would eventually take me on to Cave Hill and then on to Napoleon's Nose. We went there as kids. You could get a car right up into the old disused workings at the back. There were little huts up there, but we never saw any security in all those years. It was very private.

That was where they took Edward Campbell, a Catholic taxi driver, in 1987. They put him in the boot of his car and then they took him out and shot him up there. They would have said 'executed', no doubt. The UFF (Ulster Freedom Fighters) claimed that he was involved in intelligence gathering for the IRA. One interpretation of a man's daily habits, I suppose.

That loaded weapon of language again.

9

Somebody had built a high new metal fence up the Hightown Road that I didn't remember from the past. There was nobody about so I climbed over it to head across the rough ground. It still looked exactly as I remembered it, but I had moved on. My mother liked to remind me and everyone else of this.

'I never had to make you do your homework, you just got that wee card table out and away you went,' she would say. 'Your friends would call for you and you would have a wee chat in the hall and then you'd go back to your work.'

There was nobody pulling any strings for me, that was what she liked to say and then she would list all those boys at school who had parents in high places, at least in higher places than we did. I got three grade As at A level, a First Class degree from the University of Birmingham, and a Ph. D. from Cambridge.

I went off to Cambridge in my platform soles one bright Sunday afternoon in October. I had bought the shoes, which had red and black concentric rings around their four-inch heels, in a market under the Bull Ring in the centre of Birmingham. They were second-hand and were sold on a stall next to one that sold dirty magazines – also second-hand – that showed large white-skinned women with their legs pressed firmly together but with plenty of bush still showing.

The heel of the left shoe must have broken at some time in the past because somebody had already hammered a nail down through the inside of the shoe to keep the four-inch stack in place. They were no longer fashionable; I had bought them because they were cheap. And every now and then as I was walking along the heel would snap off, wrenching my ankle. Every time this happened I limped home and hammered another nail in.

The Sunday I went to Cambridge there were four or five three-inch nails holding the heel in and still it broke off as I ran for a bus. So I walked along the street with one leg four inches higher than the other. The heads of the nails, ragged and bent from all my hammering, had made my heel bleed through the sock. I had what must have looked like polio and a bleeding heel and a case that I couldn't carry. I dragged the case to the station like a man possessed by the devil, on my way to a new university, but I never sought any help.

I am wearing those shoes in my Freshers' photograph at Trinity College, Cambridge. I am standing among the cream of British society in Prince Charles's old college (and Edward VII's, George VI's, Earl Balfour's, Nehru's, Lord Byron's, Tennyson's, Francis Bacon's, Wittgenstein's, Bertrand Russell's, Isaac Newton's and Lord Rutherford's). There are one or two young men with titles in the row in front, one of them wearing a kilt. None of them wore platform shoes, let alone platform shoes held together with nails. My mother and I were always great ones for cheap fashion.

*

As the years passed, I moved further and further away from my roots, getting vaguer and vaguer about my past until sometimes I felt that I really had none at all, my accent changing slowly year by year. My brother and my wife – also from the turn-of-the-road area – and I all left Belfast and we all changed.

I can remember, the Christmas before he died, climbing in the Mournes with my brother in sunny, unseasonable weather. The two of us sat in a small hollow high in the Mournes, our coats off, laughing at the things my mother would say, laughing at the accents, laughing at how Van Morrison pronounces the 'a' sound in 'water' in the song 'And it stoned me', like the wee East Belfast man that he was. But secretly we liked how he said it because he was like us. My brother, wearing his ski-instructor sweaters and with his Italian sports car, was just back from Chamonix or Val d'Isère. I had my new Cambridge background. Occasionally the wee Belfast words would slip out, making us both laugh.

'Would you ever move back to Belfast?' my brother asked, and he never waited for an answer.

Our whole lives were in front of us on those bright clear mountain peaks.

I can see my brother's smiling eyes now, as he leans back. I will always have that smile in front of me, his head back in that sunlight on a bright, crisp morning. We had sandwiches with us that day; he had got up earlier than me and had made them. We had three apiece and a pint of milk between us, taking one swallow in turn until we'd drained it.

He was getting married in April, I was to be the best man, and after that he had one more expedition – to get mountaineering out of his system, he explained. He was going to the Himalalays and the mountain that he would attempt was called Nanda Devi, the Goddess of Joy. I had never heard of it.

He told me that my best man's speech had better be a good one. 'I've told my girlfriend that you're a clever wee shite, so don't let me down.'

And then, within a matter of months, no more than that, really, just months that could be counted down one by one, he had died and my wife had been dragged by her coat under a train that she had been trying to board at Sheffield station. And all the lives of our little group had changed for good, and the bright future that had seemed so clear that day had somehow dulled. That period is just a few vivid moments now. I remember two telegrams arriving simultaneously, one from my Uncle Terence saying: 'Serious accident to Bill. Ring home.'

I can't remember what the other telegram said. It was from my mother and was probably vaguer. The face of the man who delivered this telegram is just a blank in my memory. I recall the hand reaching out towards me, the movement from the bag, the two telegrams like playing cards held out in a hand in front of me, as if I could take my pick. But I had to read both and the content of one was worse than the other's.

I had started my first academic job that year in Sheffield and I lived in an old coach house, infested with rats in the loft, that crouched down below a leafy road that led towards the university from the rich suburbs where the men who had run the British steel industry had once lived such prosperous lives. I remember my heart pounding as I went to the public telephone up on the road to ring home and the question forming in my mind as I half ran and half walked along that road: 'How serious?' I was almost rehearsing it. I can remember my relief that there was nobody in the phone box: it was a Sunday morning and the streets were deserted. I must have been running towards the end when I got to the telephone and I rang my mother's number.

As soon as a quiet voice other than my mother's answered the phone, I knew exactly how serious the accident was. If my brother had been merely injured my mother would have been there on the other end of the phone, angry with him and angry with me. I had prepared myself to hear her rage. She had always hated him climbing; she never saw the point of going out into the country and into high places loaded with all that equipment. That's what she always said when the three of us were sitting in front of the fire. But this was some other woman's voice and then came a long silence filled with my dread, and then my mother's voice drowned in sobbing.

'He's dead,' she said, 'your brother's dead.'

The breaking of the worst news was as straightforward as that, that short vowel sound in the word 'dead'.

Bill was near the summit when he fell was all we ever heard. We had a service in the house though Bill's body never returned home. It lay beneath a pile of stones on a Himalayan hillside with a few details of his life scratched with a stone or an ice pick on the side of a grey slate-looking rock. 'Here lies Ben Beattie,' it read.

A few of his friends who had served their apprenticeships with him and had stuck with their trade came to the funeral; some had moved on. One was now a fireman in Belfast with stories of smoke-damaged bargains to be salvaged from shops that had been blown up. One was in insurance. Both were in professions that were now good sound businesses in

Belfast. The old house was too small and the crowd of friends and neighbours congregated on the pavement outside while some stood on the stairs.

Bill's wife of a few months was there, and she slept that night with my mother in the front bedroom. Bill would have laughed with embarrassment to hear about that. I would have loved to see his face.

'She's really middle-class,' he had told me when he and his wife-to-be had first met, and I liked the way that he had used the word 'really', as if to say that he had landed on his feet. 'I've told her about the old house,' he said, 'and she says that she understands that it's not very modern or nice, but I don't think she does.' And we both made that kind of face, like kids when they're dreading something and they want to show it. And now she was here without Bill to supervise the experience. I laughed myself at the thought of her and my mother in the same room.

Bill didn't leave much behind. He had a diary that I was allowed to look at before it was taken away from me. 'It'll just upset him,' my mother said and then she complained that I never got the clothes back that I had loaned him. She cried for months on end, every time I rang her, just as she had done for my father, although I'd had to listen to that from the back bedroom. But she always said that the loss of a child is the hardest thing to bear. 'My wee son,' was how she referred to him.

She never seemed to take in any of the details of Bill's death and still, years later, she would ask me what country he had died in. Or she would ask: 'How did he fall?' Or, 'How long was it before they found his body?' But she didn't really want an answer.

*

Five months later, my wife Carol had her accident. I saw her in the hospital the morning it happened, before they amputated her left arm, which had been crushed by the train. I can see the shine of her long dark hair on the white pillow. I had slept in after she had got up to go to Leicester for the day. She was working as a prison psychologist and had to administer a psychological test to someone on remand in a prison in Leicester. My professor's secretary had to come to my house and she knocked on the door three or four times to wake me up. She told me that Carol had had an accident, but she thought that it wasn't too serious.

'I think that she's fallen off the platform, that's all,' she said. 'Platforms aren't too high. It's not such a big fall. She'll be all right.'

I thought that she meant that Carol had fallen over while wearing her platform shoes. My mental image was of Carol tottering over on her big platforms with their four-inch black soles with red stars on them, shoes from a few years ago imported into this dreamlike sequence.

My professor was already at the hospital and stayed with me in the waiting room. As the doctor came in to talk to me I recall jumping up and hitting my head on something and wanting my injury to be serious, but it wasn't. The doctor described what had happened at the station and explained how they had to amputate the arm.

'Is there any alternative?' I asked, as if he had not considered any.

He shook his head without looking at me, and led me in to see Carol. She was conscious when I got there. She did not smile at me. Then she immediately apologized because she said that she knew what I had been going through with my brother's death.

'I'm sorry,' she said, and then she did smile a weak, half-hearted sort of smile.

I held her limp, lifeless hand in what I suppose was my pathetic attempt to show that this hand, which was to be removed, was still part of her and of us. I was wearing a white puffa jacket that my mother had bought for me that Christmas and it got smeared up and down the sleeve with Carol's blood. And when they wheeled Carol off to theatre I had to ring my mother and tell her what had happened. Her neighbours went to the chemist's to get her some tablets and she arrived later that day, keeping herself together on Valium and alcohol, after the arm had been amputated. She stared at my sleeve as if I might not have noticed the blood that was streaked right down it.

My wife never complained about what had happened to her. I always thought that this was amazing, although I never told her this to her face, and I thought that it demonstrated a great side of her Ulster Protestant character, that quiet Presbyterian determination just to get on with life no matter what happens to you, that great ability to cope with adversity. Not a bit of wonder, I thought, that Ulster Prods, or those from Ulster Protestant descent, like Davy Crockett, Sam Houston, Kit Carson, John Colter, 'Stonewall' Jackson and President Andrew Jackson shaped the history of the United States.

I like to remind myself sometimes that eleven Presidents of the United States have come from Ulster Protestant stock. How did President Theodore Roosevelt, whose people were from County Antrim, describe the Ulster Prods, called the Scots Irish in American affairs to distinguish them from the Catholic Irish? 'Strong and powerful for good and evil, swayed by gusts of stormy passion, the love of freedom rooted in their very heart's core. They suffered terrible injuries at the hands of the red men, and on their foes they waged terrible warfare in return. They were also upright, resolute, fearless, and loyal to their friends, devoted to their country. In spite of their many failings, they were of all men the best fitted to conquer the wilderness and hold it against all comers.'

In the American War of Independence, forty per cent of Washington's army were Ulstermen. And what did Washington himself say about them? 'If defeated everywhere else, I will make my last stand for liberty among the Scots Irish of my native Virginia.' Among the signatories of the Declaration of Independence five were Scots Irish, and the Secretary of the Congress, which adopted the Declaration, was an Ulsterman, Charles Thomson from Maghera, County Londonderry. The Declaration was even printed by an Ulsterman, a John Dunlap from Strabane.

My wife sometimes got depressed. 'It's only natural,' my mother said. But, as I've said, Carol never complained, and she never attempted to justify any failure to do whatever a busy and active life would require. She was twenty-five when the accident happened. She went on to bring up three children and drive and cook and sew – all with one arm – and open bottles gripped between her thighs, and hold dresses with her teeth as she pushed the needle through, and cut the family's meat that was held on boards with nails sticking out of them (boards made by her father), and play competitive badminton with me, serving and hitting the shuttlecock with her one hand until one day when some opponent protested that this was surely against all the rules of this most English of games. Somewhere it must be written in the rules, he said, that you couldn't just drop the shuttlecock and hit it with the very same hand. 'It must give you an unfair advantage.' I thought that he was joking and I am sure that I must have laughed, but he was quite serious about it. He had this sanctimonious expression on his face as if he had caught us cheating.

'But that's the English for you,' my mother said when I told her. 'They're a strange bloody people when it gets down to it.'

Carol only ever complained that she could not greet her children with her arms outstretched in the way that you should, and could not applaud when she saw them in concerts or getting prizes or running races, except by slapping her right palm down on her right thigh in a muffled sort of ritual that drew attention to itself with its oddness.

We had moved on all right, but not quite in the way that we had thought we would, that day in the sunshine in the mountains above Newcastle. And my mother stayed in Belfast, alone in her grief.

10

I passed the library on my way back to the house. The metal barrier in front of the building was twisted in on itself, suggesting that another car or lorry had been unable to stop. The library looked small, almost compressed by the years. There had been a junior library and a senior library in that small building, one room each. I wondered if it was still like that. There had once been half a shelf of books on athletics and judo and martial arts, the few things that I was interested in.

I hadn't been in the library for years, but I had heard that they had one of my books about Northern Ireland, which had been borrowed and read by local people with some interest.

'It's always out, but I don't know why,' my mother had said. 'I hate that bloody book.'

The librarian would call over to my mother's with some Agatha Christie murder mysteries and tell her that my book was out on loan again. My mother had only ever read the first chapter of *We are the People*; she said that she didn't want to upset herself any further.

Others had read my book. I already knew that. They

were not all harmless borrowers from the local library. I had been out one Eleventh Night by a bonfire in Benview, watching the little stuffed dummy that represented Robert Lundy, the military governor of Londonderry who had tried to open the gates to the army of the Catholic King James II during the siege of 1688, go up in bright orange flames. A man whom I had never met before came up to me, introduced himself and said that he had read *We are the People* and that he had enjoyed it. 'It was the most honest book about Belfast that I've read. It was a true-to-life picture,' he told me, 'and you can't be fairer than that.'

But then he had warned me that a number of his friends hadn't enjoyed my book quite so much. 'In fact, some of the people that I was in with really didn't like it at all, if you get my drift.' He had been a member of the UDA and he had been in the Maze for sixteen years or so. 'For murder,' he explained, and so had some of my critics.

'Character assassination,' he said cryptically. 'That's what they thought about your book.'

Later that same night I was walking home from the Silverstream estate and I stopped to talk to a face that I knew on some waste ground just up from the local Spar. We were just standing there in the rain, talking about old times, reminiscing about one Friday night when we were all thrown off the bus that took us home from the Starlite ballroom in the early hours because a fight had started – it may have been started by us, I can't remember.

And then another man, short and stout, appeared from nowhere. It was closing time so there were a few people heading home in ones or twos. I thought that he was just waiting for my friend to finish talking to walk home with him. He had a round face, fleshy with drink from years

100

sitting in clubs like the one he was now leaving, and no matter how hard I tried to strip away the years I couldn't recognize him at all. But he knew me.

'You're Geoffrey Beattie,' he said in an enthusiastic sort of way, rocking back onto his heels. I could smell the drink off him, so strong in my face that I turned away slightly. I smiled briefly at him, but I didn't offer him my hand because it was not a greeting you would trust, despite the enthusiasm.

'I recognized you, Geoffrey, from your photograph,' he continued and he sort of nodded at me. 'On your book cover,' he added, and I could see the smile which he had held on his face starting to fade ever so slightly, and I thought that I might be in a little bit of trouble.

'Oh,' I said, trying to put that smile back in my voice.

'Oh, yes, Geoffrey, I've heard that you've got a great sense of humour and that you're always fucking laughing. I arrived here tonight and there you were, talking to a mate of mine, laughing away as fucking usual.' He had his face right in front of mine now. 'I like a man with a good sense of fucking humour,' he said. 'I like a man who enjoys a good fucking laugh.'

I stood beside him as he fumbled in his denim jacket for something. I almost offered to help because it was taking him so long.

He took out a small heavy-looking handgun and put it to my head. 'Is that funny, then, Geoffrey?' he asked as he moved his head back round again to look me straight in the face. His friend, my old friend, tried to intervene, but the man with the gun, still maintaining eye contact, waved him away with a flick of the gun.

'No,' I replied.

'Oh, look,' he said, as if addressing a small crowd.

101

'You've stopped fucking laughing. At long last, you've stopped laughing. Now that *is* a first. You're fine as long as you've got somebody to laugh at. You're always looking down your fucking nose at us, aren't you? It's not so funny now is it? Eh?'

We stood there for a little while locked in this odd confrontation while he made his point. It was a short exchange, a practical joke for him, to be talked about later with his drinking buddies. But it seemed like a very long time to me. Then he put the gun away and his friend – because the other man was more his friend than mine after all the time I had been away, asked him why he had done that.

'I'm just making a wee point, that's all,' he said. 'Your man doesn't live here, but he thinks he's the fucking expert all of a sudden. It fucks me off.'

I stood in the drizzle with my right leg trembling intermittently, in short bursts. I pressed my heel to the ground to stop it.

'No hard feelings, mate, eh?' the man with the gun said, putting the weapon away.

'Shake hands on it,' the other man ordered and pushed us bodily towards each other.

We shook hands, and the small tubby man squeezed my hand and smiled broadly. The palm of his hand was moist with sweat, almost buttery, which surprised me. I thought that he was more in control than that.

'I had you fucking going there, though,' he said. 'You thought that your number was up.'

I tried to say that I had realized that it was all a joke, but he was having none of this.

'I could see it in your face, Geoffrey, so there's no point in fucking denying it. If one of you professors – you are a

102

professor now, aren't you? – walked shite into a room, you would stand there with the shite all over the soles of your boots still denying it. You're back home now, Geoffrey: none of that fancy talk is going to get you very far. Just remember that.'

We parted on what they saw as good terms, the two of them laughing as if they had been bonded together by my discomfort, my right leg still with a life of its own, my heart thumping in my chest. My mother was up when I got home, sitting in the kitchen, her bad ankles propped up in front of her, a few hairpins in to give her hair that curl at the front, a glass beside her, the bottle pushed out of sight behind the bread bin. I told her what had happened.

'What do you expect?' she said to me. 'I've warned you before about writing things to do with here. You want to be a bit more careful. You're all right, you don't live here. I do.' This was always her line: I wrote my stories about Belfast and then disappeared back to England. She lived among these people, her people. 'You're half English now,' she would say when she wanted to be hurtful. 'Half bloody English.' But it was still better than being just plain English, in her view.

After my mother had to retire from the mills at sixty, she was alone for large parts of the day. She came to visit us in England and she would sometimes come with me when I had to go somewhere. She had accompanied me to a television studio in Wales on one of her visits and had met Alan Whicker and Michael Fish.

'Michael Fish scratched his balls right in front of my face,' she said afterwards. 'I'll not be able to look at him in the same way again when he's doing the weather.'

And whenever I did anything in Belfast I made a point of bringing her along with me, no longer ashamed of my background like I had been when I was a student. Perhaps I was growing up. There were just a few such occasions, a few opportunities for her to see what, if anything, I had become. She came with me to hear a lecture I was giving at the University of Ulster and she proudly told me afterwards that she hadn't understood a bloody word of it, but that it sounded lovely all the same, and then she accused me of chatting up a girl in the front row.

'I've never met anybody as good at chatting up women as you,' she said. 'It must be all that psychology.'

And she accompanied me to the awards ceremony for the Ewart-Biggs Literary Prize in 1992 when *We are the People* was shortlisted. My mother had a few drinks and talked to Brian Keenan, who spoke in a whisper after all those years locked in a Beirut cellar.

'Speak up, Brian,' she kept saying. 'I can hardly hear you. Speak up, Brian, for God's sake.'

Brian kissed her when he was called forward to receive the prize for his book *An Evil Cradling*.

'He deserved it,' she said, 'for all those years sitting in the dark in that bloody cellar. He told me all about it. I told him that I knew what it was like. I never get out, either.'

We saw Andrew Motion across the room, talking to the Ewart-Biggs family. He had published my first non-academic book, *Survivors of Steel City*, a book about Sheffield, and I had drunk with him in a pub near his publishers, Chatto & Windus. I told my mother that I knew him. He nodded almost grudgingly as he passed.

'He's not a very good friend of yours, then, is he?' said my mother. 'You haven't got many good friends. I've noticed that about you. Not like when you were young.'

104

I thought of Tampy and Bill Reynolds and I smiled to myself.

We walked across town afterwards to a piano bar and my mother told the man playing the piano that it was her birthday to get a free bottle of champagne, even though it wasn't. He played 'Please Release Me' for her as a special request. Some girls at the next table on a hen night were getting a little rowdy; one wanted to kiss me because she was getting married.

'Leave him alone,' said my mother. 'He's a married man. The young hussies these days have no shame.'

A number of years later, we both went to another awards ceremony held in the Belfast City Hall. My novel *The Corner Boys* had been shortlisted for the same prize. I had been told that Chris Patten would be there to hand out the award, and that Gerry Adams would be attending the function.

'I'll have one or two things to say to old Gerry,' my mother had warned me, 'after what he's put us through. There's no two ways about that. I'll have a wee word in his ear, all right.'

She was looking forward to the event, but I was worried about what she might say; all that day she had been getting excited, talking about prize-givings of the past. 'When you and your brother were young,' she said, 'you won all the prizes in St Mark's from the JTC and the CLB. My neighbours used to tell me that it wasn't worth going because the Beattie boys won everything that was going.'

I had to get out of the house so I went shopping and then I realized that I was going to be late so I rang her from town and told her to make her own way there. I would go straight from town. So I arrived at the City Hall with my Top Shop bags, wearing a white puffa jacket just like the one I had owned years before. But this one was grey and didn't puff out very much. I had to show my invitation twice to security in order to be allowed in, and then I hung around the back door waiting for Call-a-Cab to deliver my mother.

Call-a-Cab was our local taxi firm. 'Seven and five ones,' my mother would say, 'just remember seven and five ones.' They were a Loyalist firm from the turn-of-the-road and a prime target in the days of sectarian assassination, when easy targets could just be summoned by telephone. You only had to ring the number and wait for your victim to arrive.

I had talked to one taxi driver recently whose car had been hijacked by his own side and then used in a sectarian killing. My image of the event was of this man, white and trembling and in fear of his life, bundled into the boot of another car and locked in there while the murder took place. But my image turned out to be quite wrong.

'Oh, it wasn't like that at all,' said the driver. 'The gunman just took me to a club that I knew for a wee drink. We had about five or six pints while it was all going on.'

I must have looked shocked at this account.

'I couldn't have done anything,' said the driver apologetically. 'Your man was all tooled up. He told me that it was pointless me trying to escape or raise the alarm so I might as well have a few drinks with him. We both ended up fucking well oiled. I got my car back and I was told to keep my mouth shut, or else. You don't mess with these boys, you know. You just have to go along with it, just go with the flow, and stay alive that way.'

*

106

I stood there at the back door of the City Hall and saw the Call-a-Cab car drive in past security. The driver nodded at me as if he recognized me and got my mother's wheelchair out of the boot. She was still chatting away to him. 'Do you remember playing 'foot in the bucket' when you were young?' she asked him after he had opened the door to let her out. 'That's the problem with young people nowadays, they don't know how to keep themselves amused.'

I wheeled her into the City Hall slowly and carefully. The other guests all stood around in the centre of the room, holding their wineglasses delicately. I noticed that the men all seemed to be wearing grey suits, and all the women elegant black dresses with silver brooches, and there was me in my puffa jacket and my mother in her pink anorak, with Top Shop bags balancing on her wheelchair, wearing the wig that the dog liked to chase around the house.

'I'm starving,' she said, after we had pushed through the crowd. 'I haven't had any dinner. Go and get us some of them whatever they are.'

I went in search of food and got my mother a large glass of white wine.

'I'm thirsty,' she said. 'I haven't had a drink all day.'

The speeches were starting; there were television cameras dotted around the room and every now and then some small circular area would suddenly light up in intense, white light. Chris Patten's report on the future of the RUC was just about to be released and the cameras were there partly to capture a few comments from him about the future of policing in the Province.

The other contestants and their coterie of friends stood in a group in the middle of the floor. The women in their expensive dresses adorned with silver bracelets in intricate

107

Celtic patterns looked appreciatively up at Patten. My mother was concentrating on the food in front of her. The waitress with the nibbles had found us on our own, stranded from everybody else.

'I'm starving,' my mother said to her. 'These little things don't fill you up.'

'Here you are, love,' said the waitress, handing her a larger plate as Patten started to speak.

'This is my son,' said my mother. 'He's up for the prize tonight, you know. But he won't win it. You have to be in the know to win prizes, and he doesn't know anybody.'

'Yes, but it's nice to be invited,' said the woman with the nibbles.

'Of course,' said my mother. 'That's what I tell him. You should be proud just to be invited to the City Hall.'

'Exactly,' said the waitress.

'Have you met Gerry Adams?' said my mother.

'Oh yes,' said the waitress, 'he's a regular. Him and Martin, they're never out of here – that is, when they're not up in Stormont running around as if they own the place.'

My mother was sitting in her wheelchair, making blowing noises. 'Who would have believed it?' she said. 'They're running the country and there's no two ways about that. They got everything they wanted. The Protestants got nothing.'

I stood there against the wall. I noticed that there were black stains up the outside of the arms of my jacket. I spent some time just staring at them and trying to rub them off with spit. The waitress had gone to get my mother some more wine.

'You're too backward,' my mother said to me. 'Go and talk to those men over there. Tell them that you're a professor.'

The waitress had returned with more wine and food and overheard this.

'Is he a professor?' asked the waitress.

'He is indeed. But you couldn't tell to look at him,' said my mother.

'Are those his bags?' said the waitress. 'In the old days you wouldn't have been allowed in here with bags like that.'

'Does Gerry ever try to bring big bags in with him?' my mother asked and they both started laughing. 'Is Gerry not coming, then?' enquired my mother, who I think was disappointed in some strange way.

Chris Patten looked in our direction. It was probably the laughter that attracted his attention. He said something about my novel. I couldn't hear what it was.

'What's in those mushroom pâtés?' asked my mother.

'Mushrooms,' I said.

'What else?' she asked, irritated. 'Do you know, you can't get a sensible answer out of you sometimes.'

The waitress went off to fetch some more drinks. We were still standing in the same spot. I made some pretence and then pushed my mother's chair so that she was now facing the wall, with her back to Chris Patten.

'I can't see,' she said.

'There's nothing to see,' I replied.

The waitress had returned. 'Are you not watching what's going on?' she asked. Chris Patten was just about to announce the winner. 'And the winner is . . .' he said. I didn't hear the name but I knew that it wasn't mine.

'Never mind,' said my mother.

'Never mind,' said the waitress. 'Have some more of these lovely mushroom pâtés.'

We could hear the chatter from across the room. 'What time does the bar close?' asked my mother.

'It's open as long as you like,' said the waitress. 'Within reason,' she added.

'Let's have a few more wee drinks, then,' said my mother. 'And for God's sake go and speak to some of those people. You're never going to win a prize like that if you don't speak to people,' she said. 'That's his problem: he never speaks, except to bloody women. But then, he's had a lot of practice at that.'

I wandered off to find a toilet and I tried smiling at one or two people without getting any response. My mother had decided that it was time to go.

'By the way, is there a wee phone around here for us to call Call-a-Cab when all this drink finishes?' she asked the waitress. 'We don't want to be stranded here all bloody night with nothing to eat.'

I went to ring Call-a-Cab but they were engaged, so I just hung about by the public telephone at the back door where I bumped into an attractive female TV producer from the Republic who just smiled at me and asked if I had enjoyed the proceedings. It turned out that she was there to make some arts-based programme about the shortlist for RTE, but she said that all the interviews she needed were now in the can. I blurted out, and I think that's exactly the right verb, that my book had been on the shortlist. It was too late to be relevant to anything; it was a moment for chit-chat, nothing more.

'Really?' she said, and I looked at her expression and I regretted my boast even more. 'It's a pity that we didn't get to talk earlier. Oh, here's my car – I'm just off.'

I smiled at her and walked off before doubling back to ring Call-a-Cab once more. Luckily, I got through this time.

*

I pushed my mother out into the back courtyard of the City Hall to wait for the taxi. She smiled over at the security man and he smiled back at her.

'I think that your man thinks that he's scored,' she said.

I wasn't sure whether she was joking or not, so I pretended that I hadn't heard. We hung about outside in the cold night air, a woman in a wheelchair and a man in a grubby coat. It was the professor and his proud mother going back home to the turn-of-the-road from the literary prize-giving, the professor who had abandoned his working-class roots, the professor who hadn't quite arrived anywhere else yet.

11

After *We are the People* came out, I was asked to make a documentary for BBC Northern Ireland about my old gang. But now that they were out of prison few of them were keen to appear.

'They're trying to forget the past,' said my mother. 'They're trying to move on.'

But others came forward.

So it was that one Eleventh Night at a party in the garden of a pastor in North Belfast I met Sam McCaw, who called himself Hacksaw. Hacksaw had been in the UDA and had served fourteen and a half years, mainly in the Maze, for a murder in Cambrai Street in the 1970s where a Catholic man was shot dead in front of his son, who was hit in the leg. He had joined the UDA when he was nineteen. Hacksaw seemed happy, if a little surprised, to be asked by a man with a camera about his life in the Loyalist paramilitary organization.

'I believed that what I was doing was right for Ulster and I just dedicated my loyalty to the Organization,' Hacksaw said. 'You had to do what you were told. If they came and told you that they needed you at four o'clock in the morning, you had to be there at four o'clock in the morning.'

I thought of the young lads joining the Ulster Division to march to the Somme. Hacksaw would have been about the same age and probably no less bright than many of them.

'All my friends joined the UDA as well,' he said enthusiastically. 'Instead of running about the streets, we were all in the Organization. Some of us were in prison together and I knew some of those fellas that I was in prison with better than I knew my own brothers.'

Hacksaw stood there, smiling nervously, balding now, wearing an earring and with a hood sticking like a flap out of the back of his jacket. I asked him where he got his nickname.

'It's a long story,' he said. 'It started in the Troubles when I got a bad reputation.'

'For what?' I asked.

'Bad things,' he said and he threw me an almost coy smile.

I asked him how he viewed what he had done. 'We were fighting a war against the Republican movement. They were killing the RUC, they were killing the UDR, they were killing the British Army. We are British so we had to stand up and say, 'Whoa, are we going to step back and let this happen?' We put the fear in them as well – if you're going to do that then we're going to do that to you, too. Only we'll do it harder.'

'What about that shooting in Cambrai Street? Was that someone who was targeted?' I asked.

'Well, we missed the target that night and that was the next target that came along. Instead of going home empty-handed we took him out of the picture. We weren't really looking for this one. We were looking for another one who was in the IRA. And then this other guy came along. It was denied that this one was in the IRA, but the way I see it is that throughout the Troubles if the British Army or the RUC shoot somebody then they always say that the victims were killed on active service and that they are lieutenant colonels or officer rank or they're volunteers in the IRA but when the Loyalists hit one of them – and we've got a full dossier on them – it's denied, and I believe that it's all a cover-up to make the Loyalists look as if they are just hitting ordinary Catholics.'

I asked if this was someone that they definitely had intelligence on, rather than a random Catholic.

'That was a random because we missed the one we were looking for,' he said. 'So this guy came along and we just wiped him out. I know it's sad. But that night I felt like he had to go, he just had to go. You see, we'd taken the chances of hijacking the car, going way up the Shankill with the guns in the car. We weren't going home empty-handed. Because if we had been caught we were getting big time, so he had to go, instead of us going home empty-handed.

'Cambrai Street is between the Shankill and the Crumlin. He came from the Crumlin to go across to the Shankill and we let him get to the ramps on Cambrai Street and moved out in front of him and shot him. He was in a car, his ten-year-old son was with him, but I can put my hand on my heart and say that I didn't see the child. The child was sitting on the passenger side down, but apparently the child was hit in the leg but we didn't see the child. The next day when I heard about this I wasn't worried about the father, but I was interested in the child, but when they gave it out that the child was only grazed I said, "Well, that's happy days, the child is all right." But I wasn't worried about the da because that was one less to worry about.

'Three of us went out to do the job, a driver and two gunmen. I was the driver; they both shot him. Two of us got done for it; one was never caught. We believed that once we came back from a shooting you weren't allowed to speak about it. It was loose talk then. If you were caught talking about it then you got it, so it had to be secret. If me and you and somebody else went out tonight, once we had done that mission and went back, the only ones who knew were the Commander and nobody else and that was as far as it went. You have to do what you're told, it's like if your father tells you to do something you have to do it, but it's more stricter than your father. It's hard to describe because if I don't do what I'm told then I'm putting your life in danger. And if I do something drastic while you're with me the consequences could be we could be captured or else shot dead. The adrenalin is flying through you; you're really keyed up. Capture is the last thing on your mind when you are out on a mission like that. You see, I've a gun in my hand. If somebody tries to stop us we have to shoot our way out.'

The power of language was at work again, turning Hacksaw and his two accomplices into the victims of the piece: 'We'd taken the chances of hijacking the car, going way up the Shankill with the guns in the car. We weren't going home empty-handed. Because if we had been caught we were getting big time.' He said 'empty-handed' as if they had been on some fishing trip. I watched for some recognition of the absurdity of this particular expression in his facial expression, but there was none. I listened to language with the power to transform a distance of a few hundred yards on the UDA men's home turf into a much greater one – 'way up the Shankill with the guns in the car'. And I watched Hacksaw smiling when I asked how he felt about the whole thing.

'It's sad,' he said.

The late Stanley Milgram, the American social psychologist, commented on smiles like Hacksaw's in his research on obedience. It was Milgram who conclusively demonstrated the power of the prevailing situation in producing obedience to authority. He conducted a number of psychological studies at Yale University that involved allocating experimental subjects the role of teacher in a learning task. They were told to apply what appeared to be electric shocks to 'learners' (who were, in fact, actors) when the learners made mistakes in performing tasks. Milgram found that these quite ordinary people would often continue to apply the apparent electric shocks when told to do so, to the extent of giving shocks that would – if they'd been real – have killed the learners. In fact, about sixty-five per cent of the participants in his studies continued to obey to the bitter end the experimenter who was giving the orders.

Milgram argued that crucial to such obedience is the ability of participants to offset personal responsibility for the actions by explaining them as merely instrumental, as a response to legitimate authority. I noted that Hacksaw described those giving him orders in the Organization as 'like your father asking you to do something'. Milgram also drew attention to the fact that participants would use a number of other strategies to minimize their own feelings of guilt. Some psychologists call these 'psychic blinkers', used 'to shut out the awareness that the victim is a living, suffering fellow being'. According to one of Milgram's participants: 'You really begin to forget that there's a guy out there, even though you can hear him. For a long time I just concentrated on pressing the switches and reading the words.' In a similar fashion, Hacksaw talked about his victim not by name but just as a member of a category or, rather, as a member of two overlapping categories: 'a random' and 'a Catholic'.

Interestingly, Milgram had commented on the way that individuals often smiled when they responded to the authority figure's instructions to apply the electric shocks. He had emphasized that such smiles should not be seen as smiles of enjoyment but rather as releases of tension. Was their function in the recall of such incidents essentially the same? In my own academic research I had noticed these smiles occurring in accounts of negative emotional experiences by people other than paramilitary members, and discovered that they typically accompanied some of the most negative sections of the talk itself.

I reminded myself that here in front of me was a man who had found the Lord in prison but who nevertheless still attempted to justify what he had done, the murder of a completely innocent person who had simply found himself in the wrong place at the wrong time. Not even in the wrong place at the wrong time, just going in the wrong direction in the wrong place at the wrong time – if he had been going in the opposite direction then he would have been okay because the presumption then would have been that he was a Protestant.

My mother had watched the programme that featured Hacksaw.

'They're all bloody cowboys in the UVF and the UDA

these days,' she said. 'It's not like the old days. They were definitely different then.'

'But how, exactly?' I asked. 'How were they different?'

I knew that my grandfather had been in the Ulster Volunteer Force because my mother always said that he had slept in on the day when they were landing the guns at Larne.

'Our family have always been good sleepers,' she said in his defence. 'They called for him that night but my mother couldn't wake him.'

The UVF was the armed Protestant response to Asquith's attempt to push the Home Rule Bill through the Commons. The Home Rule Bill was blocked in 1912 by the Lords, and the Ulster Unionist Council at its annual general meeting in January decided to use 'all means which may be found necessary' to stop it. The Ulster Volunteer Force was recruited from men who had signed the Ulster Covenant, pledging themselves 'to stand by one another in defending for ourselves and our children our cherished position of equal citizenship in the United Kingdom and in using all means which may be found necessary to defeat the present conspiracy to set up a Home Rule Parliament in Ireland'.

In 1914 the UDF brought arms in to Larne, Bangor and Donaghadee, weapons which were then loaded onto motor cars. In the words of the historian Jonathan Bardon, the motor cars then 'sped through the small hours, distributing them [the weapons] to prepared dumps all over the Province' – clearly without the help of my grandfather, who was fast asleep in his bed.

At other times, my mother said that her father had been involved in gun-running, although it certainly sounded as though he had missed the crucial bit. She knew that

Winston Churchill, when he was Home Secretary, had been chased from the Shankill in 1912 after he had promised that the government would introduce a Home Rule Bill in the next session 'and press it forward with all their strength'. Was her father there at that time?

'Oh, of course,' she said. 'All the men were down there giving chase; my father was always talking about Churchill being pursued down the road and having to make his speech to the Home Rulers in Celtic Park.'

Like every other Protestant in my street, I knew what had happened to the UVF when the First World War came. Edward Carson pulled his followers back from the brink of civil war with his famous telegram urging that: 'All officers, non-commissioned officers and men who are in the Ulster Volunteer Force . . . are requested to answer immediately His Majesty's call, as our first duty as loyal subjects is to the King.' The Unionist leaders unconditionally offered Lord Kitchener thirty-five thousand men and Kitchener's response was to keep the UVF together in one Ulster Division. They marched through the streets of Belfast in May 1915 and disembarked at Le Havre and Boulogne in the first days of October 1915, not knowing what lay ahead the following July.

I wasn't sure whether my grandfather was there or not. My mother's vagueness annoyed me.

'Why don't we have any souvenirs from his military past then in the house? Didn't your father even manage to bring a sword back home from India with him, ma?' asked my brother.

'He did not,' she said. 'You have to be an officer to get that sort of stuff. Ordinary soldiers like your grandfather only had little bags with them. The wee hat he brought home is all that he could carry.'

So we sat, my brother and I, gazing at this little hat. It wasn't much evidence of our heritage, let alone our *wealthy* heritage. But then, my mother had the photo, a photograph of her father George and his platoon taken somewhere tropical. They all had tans and moustaches; George was almost Indian-looking himself. They always said that there was a touch of the tar-brush about our family.

'Which one is your grandfather?' she would ask. 'Try to pick him out.' She had asked me perhaps a dozen times. I could do this without even looking at the picture. But I had to maintain the suspense. Her sister, May, would be gazing down at me.

'Let's see if he can do it, Eileen.'

I would let my hand wonder unsteadily across the page, looking at those Ulster boys out to fight for the British Empire. All sitting there, gazing at the camera, some with slight smiles. All with their tanned faces and long thin moustaches – and back in the barracks small bags with not enough space for swords or bits of a Hindu temple or large relics from some ancient civilization.

I would let my fingers hover over one or two other dark-haired lads before settling on George Willoughby. My Aunt May would laugh when I got this right. I loved her laugh. It was the most innocent laugh I have ever heard. It was a high girlie laugh and I liked to make her squeal with laughter, which wasn't that difficult.

'What did I tell you?' my mother would say. 'You always know your own. My sons always manage to pick him out from all those other men – all in the same uniform and with the same moustaches and they never saw their grandfather. George was a real Willoughby.'

'And Geoffrey might be one day,' said my Aunt May. 'Oh yes, he might be one day.'

But what had George done when he got released from the army? There were few direct answers.

'He wasn't very well,' my mother always said. Her stories were about her doing the shopping for him. He had a bad chest. She was always excusing him, as she did for my brother. 'I had to do all the running about for him.' Her own mother worked hard in the mill and George just sat about.

'His health was ruined by India,' she said. 'All those monsoons can't be good for you. He didn't like to talk about what he had been through.'

12

I had only ever really talked to one person with direct knowledge of my grandfather's generation and that was old Isaac, the barber from Ligoniel. He had walked all the way down to my mother's house one Sunday afternoon in the late 1980s when he was ninety-two years old because I had said that I wanted to speak to him for a newspaper article. At that age, he was still doing regular house calls as a barber for fifty pence and using his old hand clippers. He had worked as a barber for seventy-seven years in the same area. He could remember most of his customers – who were now pensioners – from when they were children. My Uncle Terence was one of them.

I remember Isaac's barber's shop from when I was a child. It had black and white photos around the walls, and large mirrors, and a big brush by the door for sweeping up the hair. I have an almost sensory memory of the clippers taking off the hair at the back – it was like an itch – and I find myself shivering now as I remember him tucking the gown in. Isaac didn't do neck shaves; you had to go to a more modern hairdresser at the bottom of Oakley Street for one of those. He only did short back and sides and you could either go to his shop or he came to your house. He came to our house once a month on a Thursday night and cut our hair in front of the fire: me, Bill and then my da, always in that order.

'Who's going first?' he would say, as if there was some room for negotiation.

My mother would say, 'Our Geoffrey will go first, Isaac' – the same every month.

For a man of his age Isaac was in excellent health. 'But the funny thing is,' he had told me, 'that good health doesn't run in my family.' He had been born in Bismarck Street in Ligoniel in 1896. He reminisced with me about the Ulster he had known and about the mill village of Ligoniel where he had always lived. He was a dapper little man, fiercely proud of Belfast.

'And why shouldn't I be? We had one of the greatest shipyards in the world, and some of the finest people in the world.' He remembered going down with his best friend Edward McMurray to see one of the shipyard's most famous ships being launched. 'The *Titanic* was an awful big ship,' he said, 'with four massive funnels. They said it was unsinkable, but I remember that I wasn't surprised when it went down. There was a lot of talk about it in the barber's shop for weeks afterwards.'

Isaac reminisced about the old days in Ligoniel. The history of the Province for him was a series of memories, some brief and fleeting and some more personal. You could see his eyes tracking this way and that as the images flickered in his mind's eye.

'When the original Troubles broke out in 1922, they didn't really affect Ligoniel at all. Ligoniel was a village, just like a big family – everybody knew everybody else. On the Twelfth of July, sure the Catholics would help the Protestants put the Arches up for the Orange marches to pass under. For the bonfires on the Eleventh Night, the Catholic lads would be out collecting the wood, same as anybody else.'

Isaac's loves in life were his music – 'getting the old fiddle down' – and boxing. But the photos of all the local boxers, both Protestant and Catholic, had been destroyed in the Troubles.

'When I sold up at the start of the present Troubles,' Isaac told me, 'I loaned them all to the publican from the Terminus Bar in Ligoniel. But not long after that the pub was burned to the ground, along with most of the other pubs in Ligoniel.' It sometimes seemed as if we had set about destroying our own community's past.

'But I've still got my memories of all those great fighters,' said Isaac, 'and all the local amateurs, including your Uncle Terence. Nobody up in St Vincent's club was able for him, he was too tough for any of them.' He asked me how Big Terry was and I told him that he was fine over across the water and that he had done well. 'But is he happy over there?' Isaac asked.

'I think so,' I said, 'but he misses Belfast.'

'He's bound to,' said Isaac, who had only left Belfast twice in his ninety-two years, once to go to the Isle of Man by paddle steamer and once to go to Dublin.

But Isaac also had memories of the First World War and he told me how he had tried to enlist in the 36th Ulster Division with his best friend Edward McMurray in 1914. Edward was passed as medically fit, but they wouldn't accept Isaac because he had a weakness in one leg.

'I damaged it playing football,' he said. 'I argued with them about it, I begged them to let me join up. I told them that you don't pull a trigger with your leg. But it was no good. I had to stay at home while Edward went off to war. He was a runner – he carried the messages in the 15th Battalion of the Ulster Volunteer Force. Nearly all the Ligoniel men, both Protestant and Catholic, joined the 15th Battalion. Edward fought at the Somme. He came back without one of his legs and with half a hand missing. He was in a sorry state, I can tell you. He talked about the war a lot, but the funny thing was that he never talked about the Somme. He never seemed to want to discuss the Somme itself. He used to sit in his front room, picking bits of dirt out of his good leg while he was reminiscing. The problem with his good leg was that because there were so many little wounds in it all the dirt of the day seemed to get caught in it. I used to look after it for him.'

As Isaac got up to leave that Sunday afternoon in 1988 he presented me with a shiny penny in a little tin can. It had 'Queen Victoria, Queen of England and Defender of the Faith, Empress of India' embossed on it and it had been minted in 1900. He had been polishing that penny for years. That was his gift to me. It was the shiny penny that he said his friend Edward McMurray had kept with him at the Somme for good luck.

It could, of course, have been any old coin, but I believed Isaac. He had no reason to lie to me about this. And this smooth shiny coin in my hand felt like something tangible and real from the Protestant past, as real as anything I had known. And, of course, I have lost it since. When I told my mother, she said, 'You've always been an awful careless boy.'

*

125

What was it about the Somme that Edward McMurray did not want to discuss? And what about Old Jack, one of my grandfather's drinking buddies who could hardly talk at all when he got back from the Somme? My mother and her friends used to make up jokes when they were young girls about the way that Old Jack used to blink all the time and they would laugh about how he never spoke. My mother said that he used to sit for days in his front room in front of the fire without saying a word to his wife.

'He used to just sit blinking at you when you brought his messages in,' my mother said. 'Nobody knew what was the matter with him.'

What had happened at the Somme that left some individuals so quiet and yet had such a profound and tumultuous influence on Ulster Protestant culture, so that every member of the UVF today would remind us of this older struggle in order to sanction their own actions in a very different sort of combat?

The Somme was a critical battle in the First World War because it was a deliberate and desperate attempt to break the deadlock on the Western Front. It was intended to be the one big push that would transform the whole conflict back into conventional warfare, with troop movements and strategic plans once more able to be implemented. Churchill himself commanded a battalion at the front before becoming First Lord of the Admiralty. He quotes the words of the Chief of Staff, Sir Douglas Haig, on the nature of the German defences: 'During nearly two years' preparation he [the enemy] had spared no pains to render these defences impregnable. The first and second systems each consisted of several lines of deep trenches, well provided with bomb-proof shelters and with numerous communication trenches

126

connecting them. The front of the trenches in each system was protected by wire entanglements, many of them in two belts forty yards broad, built of iron stakes interlaced with barbed wire [that was] often almost as thick as a man's finger. The numerous woods and villages in and between these systems of defence had been turned into veritable fortresses. The deep cellars usually to be found in the villages, and the numerous pits and quarries common to a chalk country, were used to provide cover for machine guns and trench mortars.'

It was against these defences that the 36th Ulster Division and others would be used. The plan was for the troops to begin their assault on 29 June at 7.30 a.m. rather than dawn to allow for better artillery observation and for the men to walk forward in waves preceded by a 'curtain' of shells to take the Schwaben Redoubt, which was to be shelled for a week beforehand in preparation for the advance. This area was named 'Devil's Dwelling' or 'Hell's Corner' by the soldiers from Ulster. It was an area protected by sixteen rows of wire before the first trench and then by five lines of German trenches, some as much as thirty feet deep. Leading the men would be officers carrying the polished blackthorn stick of the Irish regiments and – if they wished – a revolver. Philip Orr in his book *The Road to the Somme*, which describes the events of the battle as they unfolded for the soldiers in the trenches, points out that to inspire the men important objectives were given the names of Ulster towns.

The weather was good in the weeks before the battle and the soldiers themselves were aware of the beauty of the countryside. One young soldier wrote that: 'The Somme valley was filled with splendour. The mustard seed had spread a yellow carpet in many meadows, so that they were like fields of the Cloth of Gold, and clumps of red clover grew like flowers of blood. The hedges about the villages of Picardy were white with elder-flower and drenched with its scent.'

In Orr's book is a photograph of some young soldiers bathing in the River Ancre just behind the front line in the days before the battle. Out of uniform and with such carefree expressions on their faces you can see how youthful the soldiers really were. Young lads from the Shankill or the turn-of-the-road skinny-dipping in a weedy river with the flowers in bloom on the banks. It is eerie, when you know what came soon afterwards. I find myself scanning the features of these young fighters to see if I can detect anything of myself in them.

The Somme bombardment started on Saturday, 24 June and the noise of the guns could apparently be heard in London at night, 'like distant thunder'. The preparations for the advance itself continued. The plan was for the men to walk through no man's land carrying heavy backpacks. The image on the gable walls in Dunloy is not like this. On those walls the images are of men running freely towards the enemy, carrying just their rifles. At the Somme, the men actually had to set out with considerable loads on their backs. Officers were to carry a water bottle, backpack, maps, wire-cutters, an entrenching tool, a clasp knife, binoculars, a compass, mess tin, greatcoat, periscope and telescope, a revolver and four hand grenades. Privates and NCOs had a load consisting of a waterproof cape and cardigan rolled on the back of the belt, a pick or shovel, shaving and washing kit, two hand grenades – one in each side pocket – two empty sandbags tucked into the belt, a wire-cutter 'with a white tape tied round the left shoulder strap', 170 rounds of ammunition and a rifle. In addition, 'five flags for indicating the position of the most advanced infantry were to be carried by each company'.

Then the weather turned bad and the advance was delayed for a couple of days. It was time to reflect and to write home in sombre mood. One member of the Young Citizens' Volunteers wrote to the secretary of his Orange Lodge near Portadown. 'There is no doubt that when you receive this note I shall be dead. There are all the signs that something bigger than has ever taken place before in this war is about to be launched. The more I brood on what may happen the surer I am [that] I shall not survive it. All of us say, "It'll be the other fellow who'll be killed." I feel that I am one of those other fellows.'

Another wrote: 'The only thing I can compare it with is like waiting for someone to die. You know it's coming and you wish to God it was over and done with.'

At 1.10 a.m. on Saturday, 1 July the timing of zero hour was passed on to all the officers assembled in the trenches. Orr says that some men slept fitfully for short periods that night, but there would have been little real sleep for anyone.

At 4.00 a.m. dawn broke, and some battalions had an Ulster fry and some strong sugary tea to energize them for battle.

At 6.25 a.m. the final British barrage opened up, and one soldier observed that 'the air hummed like a swarm of a hundred million hornets'. The early mist was clearing. Some knelt and prayed. The traditional issue of rum was distributed, but since many men in the 36th Ulster Division were teetotal others got double or triple the usual amount. I can imagine it being passed along. I can almost hear the words themselves. I suppose this is the test of whether it's your history or not. 'Yer man's good living, I'll have his.' I can hear those words. 'Good living,' that's what they would have said. 'He's a good-livin' fella,' they would be saying. 'I'll have his, if he doesn't want it.'

Orr writes that: 'Some men had picked wild flowers and placed them in their tunics ... yellow charlock, blue cornflowers and crimson poppies. Some had even acquired orange lilies.' But these words were really taken from Michael MacDonagh's book *The Irish at the Somme*, published in 1918. A Member of Parliament, John Redmond, wrote the foreword and describes how MacDonagh continued his 'thrilling story begun in *The Irish at the Front*'. The book opens with some descriptions of how the soldiers of the Connaught Rangers, when hearing that they were to march, in 'jubilation, danced Irish jigs and reels and sang national songs'. It was MacDonagh who originally described how the men had brought the orange lilies with them.

I am a little sceptical about this, as I am about 'jigs and reels' and the devil-may-care attitudes of the fighting Irish. And I can't see the flowers somehow or the men pinning them singly or in bunches to their tunics.

According to Orr some of the men had brought their Orange sashes with them and they now started to put them on. MacDonagh mentions this as well, but in his book it is not portrayed as such a widespread practice. 'One sergeant of the Inniskillings went into the fray with his Orange sash on him,' MacDonagh wrote. Still, it is part of the iconic representation of the Protestants at the Somme.

In his play *Observe the Sons of Ulster Marching Towards the Somme*, Frank McGuinness writes: '*Anderson*: We've noticed something missing from your uniform. Something important. We think you should do something about it. It might get you into trouble. *Pyper*: What's missing? *Anderson*: Your badge of honour. (Anderson hands out an Orange sash to Pyper.)'

But I can imagine this more easily: the men getting the folded sashes out of their backpacks, their most precious possession, the one thing that would identify them in that blackened earth. Then dressing for death, each soldier adjusting his neighbour's sash, as if they were going to the Field for the last time.

In the last few minutes before setting off to walk behind a curtain of falling shells into no man's land, according to Orr, short comforting parts of Orange Lodge meetings were held. You can imagine a few prayers, said quietly to cover the fear in the men's voices. There are old photographs of the men of Ulster on their knees praying before the advance.

The Catholics in the 36th Ulster Division, whose presence that day is often overlooked, got the opportunity to attend Mass on the day before the battle.

At 7.10 a.m. on 1 July 1916 the first Ulstermen climbed over the parapet of their trench and lay down in long lines. Then, five minutes later, the second wave climbed out and lay down, and then the third five minutes after that, all waiting for the bombardment to cease. At 7.30 a.m. the whistles of the officers sounded and the men rose to their feet and started to walk forward.

The war correspondent of *The Times* wrote: 'When I saw the men emerge through the smoke and form up as if on parade, I could hardly believe my eyes.'

As the leading soldiers neared the first German line there were cries of 'No surrender, boys!' I can hear that in my head.

MacDonagh has them shouting other encouragements as

well: '"Let her rip, ye devils!" shouted some of the Ulstermen in jocular fashion at the enemy and his machine-gun . . .' he wrote. '"Come on, boys, this is the first of July." "No surrender!" roared the men.'

The casualties were appalling but the 36th Ulster Division still managed to break through the first four lines of trenches until they were virtually surrounded, exposed as they now were in such a forward position.

'We got into what must have been at one time a German trench and waited for the rest to catch up with us but they never came. We could see nothing but Germans all around us. When we were in the old German trench . . . a sergeant asked us if we wanted to surrender. "No surrender" was the shout. "No surrender. No Home Rule. For God and Ulster."' (P. Orr, *The Road to the Somme: Men of the Ulster Division Tell Their Story*).

What did they say about their walk through the valley of death? 'There was fellas crawlin' back that couldn't walk. One fella lay down, put down his rifle, covered himself with his groundsheet and when we came across him he was dead. No one to touch them. I used to think it was terrible to see young lives – the blood of life oozing out of them. Nobody there to lift their head – not one – nobody there to care – that was it.' (Orr, *The Road to the Somme*)

By the time night fell, there had been nearly sixty thousand British casualties and prisoners of war. Twenty thousand died. 'This was the greatest loss and slaughter sustained in a single day in the whole history of the British army,' Churchill wrote. He added, with a hint of melancholy: 'By the evening of July 1, the German 180th Infantry Regiment

132

was again in possession of the whole of its trenches.'

The 36th Ulster Division sustained terrible losses. I had always thought of the Somme as a battle fought just by Protestant Ulster on the British side but a table in Churchill's book reminds one of the other sections of the army that also suffered severe casualties: the Middlesex Regiment, the Devons, the West Yorks, the Berkshire, the Lincoln, the York and Lancaster and the Sherwood Foresters. Churchill neatly summarized the statistics of battle, comparing losses among the officers with those among the other ranks. Ulster suffered but so did many other British regions. And from further afield, the 1st Newfoundland Regiment took ninety-five per cent casualties.

On Tuesday, 11 July, when what was left of the 36th Ulster Division left Picardy, they had suffered over five thousand casualties, and over two thousand killed. The next day, on the march to Blaringhem, it was reported that some of the men saw small orange flowers growing by the roadside and they were given special permission to break ranks to collect these flowers for their tunics as the band played 'King William's March'.

As a boy I had read Michael MacDonagh's *The Irish at the Somme*, with its alarming green, black and white cover showing the Irish soldier holding the flag with an Irish harp on it. But it was only the chapter on 'The Exploits of the Ulster Division' that interested me then and the comments of the unnamed British officer on the conduct of the 36th Ulster Division, which the original UVF had become. 'I am not an Ulsterman, but as I followed the amazing attack of the Ulster Division on July 1, I felt that I would rather be an Ulsterman than anything else in the world. With shouts of

"Remember the Boyne" and "No surrender, boys", they threw themselves at the Germans, and before they could be restrained had penetrated to the enemy fifth line. The attack was one of the greatest revelations of human courage and endurance known in history.'

I get a little weepy when I read these lines, although I'm not normally that emotional an individual.

13

Edward McMurray, whose good-luck penny I'd received, would never have seen the flowers at the side of the road on the way back from the Somme, nor would he have heard the Orange tunes again as they marched past those fields of flowers. He would have seen the inside of a field hospital and he would have experienced the sights and sounds inside those long tents with their rows upon rows of the helpless dying.

Military historians tell us that by mid-November 1916 the Allies had advanced five miles at a cost of 450,000 German, 200,000 French and 420,000 British casualties. But to glimpse the real cost of the Somme you have to travel back to Belfast and those little streets off the Shankill and in Ligoniel.

Small buff-coloured envelopes began to arrive at the doors of the houses in the narrow mill streets of Belfast. Philip Orr describes how the Mabins of the Shankill had two boys in the army and one day the postman had two envelopes for Mrs Mabin. But he just couldn't face the prospect of delivering both at the same time so he held one back until later. I can imagine Mrs Mabin waiting in the kitchen day after day, washing the dishes and listening out for that loud knock that she knows will make her jump no matter how prepared she is.

And then one day she can see the postman out the front, standing there. Even before he raps the door her heart is in her mouth. I can see her kitchen and its damp, slimy walls, with a fire in the front room and a rusty tin bath hanging from the nail on the yard wall. I can hear her voice.

'Oh Jesus,' she says. I know how that voice sounds. It's my mother's voice. 'Oh, Jesus, no.' She makes her way through the front room, brushing against the chair. It's a small cramped room – I can see the furniture, I know where she would have got it. She's already crying quietly, and she opens the front door so that she has to step back to get past. It's summer, there's a flag up outside, it's the Union Jack, and some orange bunting, limp from the rain of the past few days. It's always wet in July.

The postman is holding something out in front of him: he doesn't say anything, his face is just a blur. Mrs Mabin reaches out her hand and you can almost see the postman trying to draw the envelope away at the last minute.

Her next-door neighbour is out on the street; she heard the knock. 'Oh Rosemary,' she says. 'Oh Jesus, Rosemary, not one of your sons,' and she rushes out and puts her arm around her neighbour.

The postman doesn't move and he doesn't say anything. Mrs Mabin opens the envelope slowly. She wants to see the name, and for a second the postman feels ashamed. 'It's my Davy, my wee son,' she says. And both women start to sob, but not openly on the street – they go inside for that. Her neighbour thanks the postman; she would do that for her friend. And the postman walks off fingering the other envelope for Mrs Mabin, the envelope lying on its own at the bottom of his bag and he dreads having to come back later that day. But he knows that he must.

I think about the men returning without their friends, guilty to be alive, haunted with the images of war during the days and in the long restless nights, sitting alone, quiet in front of the fire, bursting into tears suddenly and without explanation. And their mothers trying to understand, for months trying to understand but not being able to, and then getting angry at the boys, taking their anger out on them.

And then later a mother, any mother saying to the neighbour, right in front of her lad, 'He's a changed boy. He was always so happy-go-lucky before, such a happy wee child before he had the arm off.' Sometimes, turning to their changed son: 'You'll have to pull yourself together. This isn't doing you any good, you know.' A mixture of fear and confusion and that kind of self-protective anger in these voices.

I can see the stump of the arm with muscle and gristle, pink and throbbing, the skin graft from the thighs leaving big purple bruises down there. He doesn't wear anything over the stump. He just leaves it poking out of short-sleeved shirts in the summer. I can see the shoulder of the amputated arm withering over the months and the years, until it is like the shoulder of a child. I can see the sly, unforgiving looks of strangers at the empty sleeve.

Sometimes the returning heroes might talk a little, reminding themselves of their last conversations with their dead friends. 'I said that when it was all over we were going to go down to Bangor for the day and go out on a wee boat and just put our feet up and smoke all day long.'

Not great romantic ambitions, just something that I can imagine might have come to them on that morning when they were lying in those great long lines before marching with heavy packs on their backs through the blackened earth. An image of a rowing boat off Pickie Pool in the one good day of summer somewhere at the front of their mind.

And the mother looking down at her wee boy, his face lit up the light of the fire flickering on it, old now before his time, sitting flicking his ash into the fire, some getting on his trousers. 'But I never gave him the fag I owed him. Billy died without me ever getting the chance to pay him back.'

And the mother not knowing what to do, except get a little angry with her son for being like this. 'You can't sit there for the rest of your life, you know,' she would shout from the kitchen. 'We've all got to move on.'

Of course, there were some lucky ones, who came back and found that they could talk about what they had experienced to their wives, to their children, to whoever might listen. I recall the start of Michael Longley's poem about his father, 'Wound'.

> Here are two pictures from my father's head –
> I have kept them like secrets until now:
> First, the Ulster Division at the Somme
> Going over the top with 'Fuck the Pope!'
> 'No surrender!' a boy about to die,
> Screaming, 'Give 'em one for the Shankill!'
> 'Wilder than Gurkhas' were my father's words
> Of admiration and bewilderment.

It was something to live up to for those of us who came later. MacDonagh also shares with us more thrilling tales from the Front from those who returned. 'The Huns turned on them like baffled tigers and tried to hurl the Irishmen out again, but they might as well have tried to batter down the walls of Derry with toothpicks.' We were already sculpting our romantic past. The line from Longley's poem – 'Give 'em one for the Shankill!' – is close to a shouted retort in MacDonagh's book: 'Give them it hot for the Shankill Road.' Anything that reminds me of MacDonagh's book I find disquieting, and yet I find comfort in the fact that two officers and two privates of the 36th Ulster Division won Victoria Crosses for exceptional gallantry. That cannot be taken away. There were heroes in our streets, all right.

Yet there is more to the record of the Somme than the statistics and the fleeting heroic stories that were told and retold and became our history. The Somme was more than a few months in France for those who survived, and there was more to it than this for our culture. It seems that veterans like Edward McMurray and Old Jack, my grandfather's buddy, were not alone in their silence. Many of those who came back from the trenches said nothing, sometimes quite literally nothing at all. A decade after the end of the war, thirty-six per cent of the veterans receiving disability pensions from the British government were psychiatric casualties of combat. My mother always said that her father's drinking friends never spoke about it and one of his best friends hardly spoke at all.

Shell-shock was prevalent among the troops returning from the conflict and the commonest symptom of that great disorder of the First World War was mutism, particularly among the 'other ranks'. The soldiers quite simply couldn't speak any longer, even when they tried.

Shell-shock precipitated something of a crisis in the medical profession in the 1920s because suddenly men were suffering from forms of hysterical disorder, that is to say disorders with no organic cause that had previously been thought to afflict mainly women, and veterans were presenting with these disorders in numbers such as had never been seen before. Eric Leed in his book *No Man's Land* comments that: 'The symptoms of shell-shock were precisely the same as those of the most common hysterical disorders of peacetime though they often acquired new and more dramatic names in war: "the burial-alive neurosis", "gas neurosis", "soldier's heart", "hysterical sympathy with the enemy". True, what had been predominantly a disease of women before the war became a disease of men in combat.' The question was why.

A predecessor of mine at the University of Manchester, T.H. Pear, the first full-time Professor of Psychology in this country, suggested in his book written with G. Elliot Smith entitled *Shell-Shock and Its Lessons* that it was not just the routine horrors of war that were responsible for this but the peculiar psychological conditions of trench warfare. There were certain features of this kind of warfare that made the experience particularly damaging, namely the unpredictability of the unseen enemy shelling from a distance and the fact that any kind of direct physical response such as a counter-attack was often not possible. Pear and Smith argued that this was particularly psychologically damaging: 'One natural way is forbidden [the soldier] in which he might give vent to his pent-up emotion, by rushing out and charging the enemy. He is thus attacked from within and without.' It was the passivity of trench warfare, as much as

140

anything else, combined with intense fear and anxiety that was the root cause of the disturbance.

Leed, reviewing the evidence much later, commented that: 'The most significant variable in the incidence of neurosis was not the character of the soldier but the character of the war. When the war again became a war of movement with the German offensive of 1918, even though the fighting was intense and exhausting, the incidence of war neurosis dropped dramatically.'

Smith and Pear argued for the importance of psychological factors in the development of shell-shock, but the medical establishment of the time did not agree. These were considered dangerous, even subversive views. How was one to distinguish shell-shock, a hysterical disorder with no identifiable organic cause, from cowardice or shirking? There was a vitriolic exchange in the pages of the science journal *Nature* between Smith and Pear on the one hand and Sir Robert Armstrong-Jones, who represented prevailing medical opinion and who had reviewed their book in the journal concerned, on the other. In science we sometimes talk of scientists contesting their views, but here the nature of the contest was not metaphorical. This was a life-and-death struggle for the souls of the soldiers. Armstrong-Jones maintained (6 September 1917) that, contrary to the views of Smith and Pear, shell-shock was mainly due to physical causes, particularly 'physical weariness, fatigue, exposure, insomnia, exhaustion, and irregular meals – possibly also on occasion malaria and venereal disease' acting on those with 'a family history of insanity, epilepsy, paralysis, neurasthenia, or parental alcoholism . . . at any rate . . . some deeply ingrained defect only curable by extinction of the stock or by its repeated crossing with other more stable stocks'. According to this

141

interpretation, those mute boys from Belfast and Yorkshire who had suffered extreme fatigue and exposure, unable to sleep because of the constant shelling, had some essential defect in their genetic make-up.

Armstrong-Jones's eugenicist argument may seem a little odd now at the start of a new century where we accept more readily the role of psychological factors in illness. But then the role of the mind was much less well understood. The commonest treatments for shell-shock, during and immediately after the First World War, were a variety of what Leed labelled 'disciplinary' therapies. The leading advocate in Britain of such remedies was Lewis Yealland, who pioneered the use of electric shock treatment.

Yealland describes his treatment of a typical shell-shock case, a twenty-four-year-old private who had been totally mute for nine months. This soldier had survived the retreat from Mons, the battle of the Marne, the battle of the Aisne, and the first and second battles of Ypres, among others. Having been sent to Salonica to take part in the Gallipoli expedition he collapsed from what he said was the heat and woke up totally mute: 'for five hours he remained unconscious and on waking "shook all over" and could not speak.'

Yealland outlines his particular therapeutic approach: 'In the evening [the soldier] was taken to the electrical room, the blinds drawn, the lights turned out and the doors leading into the room were locked and the keys removed. The only light perceptible was that from the resistance bulbs of the battery. Placing the pad electrode on the lumbar spine and attaching the long pharyngeal electrode, I said to him, "You will not leave this room until you are talking as well as you ever did; no, not before." The mouth was kept open by means of a tongue depressor; a strong faradic current was applied to the posterior wall of the pharynx, and with this stimulus he jumped backwards, detaching the wires from the battery. "Remember, you must behave as becomes the hero I expect you to be," I said. "A man who has gone through so many battles should have better control of himself." Then I placed him in a position from which he could not release himself, and repeated, "You must talk before you leave me."

Electricity was then applied for one hour, at the end of which time the patient could apparently whisper the sound 'ah'. Yealland was obviously pleased with the progress. Yealland reports that he said to the soldier: 'Do you realize that there is already an improvement . . . Small as it may seem to you, if you consider rationally for yourself, you will believe me when I tell you that you will be talking before long.' After two hours, the patient tried to get out of the room but was prevented from doing so. The control of the situation resided entirely with the therapist. Yealland writes that he said to the patient, 'When the time comes for more electricity you will be given it, whether you wish it or not.'

Yealland was using an extreme form of aversion therapy, one type of behaviour modification, to work on the particular symptoms, whether they were mutism, involuntary movements or disorder of vision. There was no attempt to understand what the individual had been through. The focus was merely on changing his behaviour and even when the mutism had been 'cured' by the application of strong electrical currents in a darkened room from which escape was impossible, until the sound 'ah' was whispered again and again and again, or until the patient could whisper 'ah', 'bah', cah' over and over on Yealland's request, or until the patient had replaced the nightmares of the filthy trenches of the Somme with nightmares of the

143

horrors of Yealland's treatment room – even then Yealland quite explicitly did not want them to confide or discuss or remember what they had been through. He wrote: 'With recovery of the voice there is usually a marked change in the mental condition of the patient . . . He will confide in you, and as a rule becomes very demonstrative. At times he will break down emotionally as he refers to his previous hardships; all this, however, can be easily controlled by one who is ordinarily inventive. The hand-shake must be refused and he must not be allowed to think that a miracle has been performed. The patient is not sent back to his ward until he has been cured; all references to his former condition are discouraged.'

The human cost of the Battle of the Somme was tremendous. Young men, some very young indeed, were exposed to a situation such as had never been seen before. The human nervous system was not adapted to this new form of warfare where in many circumstances neither fight nor flight was possible, and the outcome was a breakdown in movement, in speech, in general human functioning.

These young men were then transported back to England and electric currents were put through them until they made sounds and more electricity was put through them until they said words and the cure was considered effected. Effected by a therapist who warned them not to reflect on what had happened, who would not shake their hand, who would not allow any emotion to be displayed in this darkened room where this crude barbaric, behavioural science held sway.

But there was an alternative to the darkened rooms of Yealland, at the more civilized setting of Craiglockhart Military Hospital near Edinburgh, the hospital described in

Pat Barker's novel *Regeneration*, where the therapist was the renowned Dr W. H. R. Rivers. The patients tended to be officers and included, among others, both Second Lieutenant Siegfried Sassoon and Wilfred Owen.

Rivers pioneered at Craiglockhart the talking cure with, it must be said, articulate and sensitive young officers who were now for the very first time given the opportunity to talk about their experiences in the war. Officers who had previously been told that it was their duty to forget such experiences and, as befitted men of this social class, in Rivers's own words had done their 'utmost in this direction'.

Rivers details how he talked some of these young officers through their experiences. For example, one man who was buried alive after a shell exploded near him had symptoms including severe headache, vomiting and problems in urinating. This officer had apparently remained on duty for a further two months following this particular experience before collapsing altogether after 'he had gone out to seek a fellow officer and had found his body blown into pieces, with head and limbs lying separated from the trunk.' This man's nights were haunted by dreams of his dead and mutilated friend. Sometimes the friend appeared in his dreams as he had seen him in the field that day, but sometimes the dead officer appeared with his limbs and his features eaten away by leprosy. The young officer dreaded going to sleep at nights: the expert medical advice that he received at the time was that he should merely attempt to banish all thoughts of his young comrade from his mind. This medical advice exacerbated the problem because, in Rivers's words, 'there is no question but that he was striving by day to dispel memories only to bring them upon him with redoubled force and horror when he slept'.

Rivers's evolving therapeutic-intervention technique

was to allow the young officer to talk about what he had experienced and for Rivers to draw attention to important features of the experience, in this case that the mangled state of the body was conclusive evidence that his friend had been killed outright. This helped the patient enormously, according to Rivers, because he could then provide his own narrative about what had happened to his friend and take some comfort from the fact that the dead man had not suffered like many of the other casualties. He was no longer having to banish the thoughts and memories of the other officer from his mind, and the therapeutic outcome was that for several nights the patient had no dreams at all. Then, when he did dream about his comrade again, the experience did not have the same horror attached to it. This patient, according to Rivers, made a good recovery and was finally able to talk about what had happened to his friend.

Rivers, in contrast to Yealland who was punishing those suffering from shell-shock by attempting almost physically to drive the symptoms out of them, was trying to induce some sort of cure. Rivers says that for those individuals who have been brooding over their painful thoughts, 'In such cases the greatest relief is afforded by the mere communication of these troubles to another.' This was seen as a very radical form of therapy at the time. And perhaps for the first time the remembering of past events, the effort to encode images into words and hence resolve them into meaning was seen as being of therapeutic value rather than something to be avoided at all costs.

Reading about shell-shock and its victims gave me a different understanding of the events at the Somme. The stories that the patients and their therapists provided allowed a different sort of insight into what life in the trenches had really been like. There were many brave men who fought and died at the Somme and many more, in fact hundreds of thousands more, who had to try to live with the shame of their particular neurotic response to the unpredictability of violent death inflicted by an unseen enemy during periods of enforced passivity. These responses were quite natural reactions to a situation where the normal human impulses of fight or flight, which form the very core of our biological being, were blocked. And if the soldiers did crack under this pressure, there was little human understanding waiting for them in hospital back in England, unless they were very privileged to begin with. Those who could talk about the Ulster Division being 'wild like Gurkhas' at the Somme were truly the lucky ones.

It took nearly another seventy years before we fully recognized the significance of all of this. There is now a vast amount of evidence, in both the psychological and medical literatures, that indicates that traumatic experiences can give rise to mental and physical health problems. The famous American psychologist James Pennebaker put forward in 1982 a psychological theory of inhibition that summarized the processes by which failure to confront traumatic events can result in poorer health. The principal assumption of this theory is that the inhibition of thoughts, feelings, and behaviour is an active process that involves intense physiological strain. Pennebaker reviews the evidence that when the desire to talk about negative experiences is inhibited over long periods of time aggregated stress is placed on the body, which results in increased susceptibility to stress-related diseases, including cancer and high blood pressure as well as other physical ailments.

Pennebaker suggested that: 'Through language

individuals are able to organize, structure and ultimately assimilate both their emotional experiences and the events that may have provoked the emotions.' I have conducted some research into this question with a Ph.D. student, Vicky Lee, and analysed in detail exactly what people talk about when they are encouraged to discuss negative or traumatic events and their reaction to them. One of the central aspects of such accounts is the way in which the individual attributes responsibility for the event itself and their emotional response to it. It is not just a case of individuals 'organizing, structuring and assimilating their emotional experiences' of the events themselves but the negotiation of their own personal responsibility – and the blame and responsibility of others – for the sequence of things that happened and their psychological response to them that appears to be crucial. This is a central part of what it is to understand an event, the comprehension of why it occurred. The reason why it is so good to talk about traumatic or negative events is that we get the opportunity to work out our own role, if any, in the development of these events and this role needs to be constructed in talk, using all the complex devices that language provides us with: the vocabulary, the syntax and the causal connectives like 'because' and 'since', 'thus' or 'why', that bind a linguistic account together. Thoughts running around in our head that are never properly articulated do not allow the event or events to be properly understood; they do not specifically allow issues of responsibility to be properly resolved.

Many of those who came back from the Somme never got the chance to do any of this constructive talking. They never got the chance to talk about why their friend died instead of them, or why the fact that they did not react quickly enough on sentry duty caused the warning of that particular attack to be delayed for a few precious seconds, or why the officers who gave the orders to march forward in lines across no man's land were operating with a logic all of their own, and how this logic didn't make sense to the ordinary individual soldier. We now know what the suppression of all these kinds of thoughts can do to the human body and I think that it gives a clue as to why so many working-class families in Belfast have never known their grandparents and why the cultural history of this group, which should have been passed down orally through the generations, is so short and so vague. Too many of those who survived the Somme died young of cancer and bad hearts without ever talking about it, keeping their secrets to themselves.

Of course, I can't think about disclosure and inhibition without recalling Hacksaw and remembering that here was a man quite able to talk about what he had done. Hacksaw and those like him are unlikely to suffer the same negative physical consequences of stress-related diseases in the years ahead. They and their memories, which will become our folk memories, are likely to be about for some considerable time to come. And sometimes that, I think, is an equally frightening thought.

PART III

THE TURN OF THE ROAD

14

After my weekend visit to my mother I became keen to look more closely into our family's history. I started visiting Belfast more frequently, and one afternoon I took my mother up to the General Records Office and scanned the Belfast Street Directories for the dates just before and just after the First World War, to settle once and for all what George's connection with the Somme might have been.

There was a lot of important information in those yellowed pages. In 1918 George Willoughby had lived in 15 Legmore Street; he was at that time a 'rougher' in the linen industry. A J. Donaghy had been our next-door neighbour then; he was a rougher as well and a Catholic, and presumably the father of the Joey Donaghy that I knew as a child. An R. Rock lived at number 11; he was another Catholic. This Mr Rock was a labourer and the father of John Rock, the Mr Rock that I knew. In 1914 at the start of the war George was there in number 15, and Joey was next door, but in number 11 lived a Joseph Baker. The Rocks, in other words, had moved into Legmore Street during the First World War.

It was odd to see this written down, and strange to see

my history bound up with these other families whom I had always known, the Catholic families that I had grown up with as a child. The Rocks had to leave their house during the Troubles because one night somebody took a shot at a man down at the turn-of-the-road and then, it was said, this gunman had escaped by running into the Rocks' house and over their yard wall. So the following night somebody fired into the Rocks' house. Nobody was injured but the Rocks moved to the top end of Ligoniel, 'to be with their own kind' as my mother put it. She meant other Catholics.

In 1914 there were ten labourers, four mill workers and one butcher in Legmore Street, Protestant and Catholic all living together and doing the same kind of work. So much for the Protestant ascendancy that I had been criticized for repeatedly by my trendy English middle-class socialist friends during my time at university, when being an Ulster Protestant was one of the worst things that you could be, as bad as being a white South African. The Protestants, they said, had prospered by exploiting their poor Catholic neighbours.

The Belfast Street Directories even informed me when George got out of the army. In 1909 he is in Legmore Street and he is there in 1907 but in 1906 Mary Willoughby, George's wife and my grandmother, is in 4 Barginnis Street. So George must have got out of the army at about this time and moved to a new house. In 1907 numbers 17–25 in Legmore Street are all vacant and there is no record for Legmore Street in 1905. So you get the impression that this was when the old house was built and that Mary lived in an adjacent street for years. She is named as the householder in Barginnis Street in 1899. Whatever wars George had served in were earlier than the Somme.

*

Although the Street Directories may appear to be dry registers of household names they do, in fact, record the comings and goings of the householder: they tell you when the man of the house went away and when he returned, and more besides. When we were young the reedy dam at the top of Ligoniel, which was always considered the most treacherous of all the dams in the area, the one rumoured to have taken several young lives, was called Bodel's Dam. Nobody seemed to know why it was called this. But I now discovered that James Bodel had been the spinning master in Ligoniel in the late nineteenth century. At the turn-of-the-road there was always an O'Hara's shop and an O'Hara's bakery. W. J. O'Hara was a matchmaker in Ligoniel in 1877. And the Ewart family, who owned the mills in Ligoniel, were there, living in Glenbank House, at the same time. The Belfast that I knew as a child had been laid down a hundred years before with the capitalist classes and the workers firmly in their places. George might have been an Orangeman but he worked cheek by jowl with his Catholic neighbours when he got out of the army.

My mother's maternal grandfather was called Nocher, sometimes spelt 'Nocker', and there was a Thomas Nocker working in Ligoniel as a reeling master and living in Bellevue Terrace in the nineteenth century and a Thomas Nocher working as a store man and living at 29 Ligoniel Road in 1914. There was also a John Nocher working as a groom and living in Roy Street in the Cromac area in 1870. All the times that I had heard the Dunville Story I had never enquired which side of my mother's family was meant to be connected to the Dunvilles – her father's or her mother's. John Nocher might indeed have worked as a groom on a large estate like the Dunvilles' and might indeed have got some innocent girl into trouble. Alternatively, he might have just been an employee whom the family went to see one afternoon, and that one solitary visit from the titled classes could have formed the basis of our family's oral history for the generations since.

I knew that 'Beattie' was a Scottish surname, although recently I had been surprised to discover that there was some dispute about this. One source told me that it was mainly the name of Scottish settlers in Ulster, whereas in other parts of the country it was the Anglicized form of 'Biadhtach', which is Gaelic for public victualler (meaning one who held land on condition of supplying food, 'biad', to those billeted on him by the chief). This still existed in the Athlone area of the Irish Midlands as an occupational surname. However, according to Black's authoritative text *Surnames of Scotland: Their Origin, Meaning and History* there is no evidence to support this theory that 'Beattie' is Gaelic in origin. According to Black, it is quite unambiguously Scottish and is a well-known Border surname, 'from Bate or Baty, pet or diminutive forms of Bartholomew'. The name was found in Berwick-on-Tweed as early as 1334, as well as further north: 'The surname is also found early in the north, where we find John Betty admitted burgess of Aberdeen in 1473.' In the eighteenth century the name was apparently common in the parish of Laurencekirk: 'nearly every farm in the parish was at one time or other in the hands of a Beattie' (Fraser, *History of Laurencekirk*).

Another account of the name can be found in John O'Hart's account of Irish pedigrees, *The Origin and Stem of the Irish Nation*. This is a slightly more fanciful account, but I took note of it because it starts with a description of the 'Beattie stem of the Irish nation' with the name 'Goffrey (or Jeffrey) Beattie'. O'Hart (1892) cites the work of Tipper who wrote a text on Irish pedigrees in the Irish language in 1713, in which he says that 'Goffrey, one of the princes from Scotland, who siding with the Irish Monarch Brian Boru, fought at the battle of Clontarf, in 1014, was the ancestor of Betagh, modernized Beattie, Beatty, Beaty, Beytagh, and Battie.'

My father called me 'Geoffrey' not because of Prince Goffrey Betagh who had fought with Brian Boru at the Battle of Clontarf but because of Geoffrey Duke, the motorbike rider. My father needed to think of a name quickly because the doctors did not expect me to survive the birth and according to my mother they needed a name for the death certificate. It was all that my father could come up with quickly. He tended to get flustered at times like that, according to my mother.

I knew that my father's family came from the Dromore area and that at least gave me some hint as to where to look for the roots of my family in pre-industrial Northern Ireland. I scanned the documents known as *Griffith's Primary Valuation*, which details the general valuation of all rateable property in Ireland in the period from 1824 to 1860. I wasn't really expecting to find anything because it already seemed that I was descended from a long line of working men and women. But there in the Union of Banbridge in the County of Down was a Sam Beatty in the townland of Drumaknockan with twenty-two rateable acres in 1834, twelve of them being first class.

My response to this discovery was almost visceral. If my father was born in 1914, and my grandfather some time, say, in the 1880s, my great-grandfather in the 1850s, then this Sam Beatty of Drumaknockan must have been my great-great-great-grandfather, working the soil of Ireland at the time when the white man was crossing the Rockies for the first time, led by the sons of Ulstermen like Kit Carson and John Colter.

Like a child again, I rushed out to the other room where my mother sat huddled in her coat. 'How much longer are you going to be?' she said. 'It's freezing in this place.'

I told her what I had found out about Sam Beatty but she seemed not that interested.

'What about the Dunvilles?' she asked.

I mentioned John Nocher the groom and a possible explanation of why the Dunvilles might have visited an ex-employee but she seemed more than a little disappointed and got a little defensive.

'It was only a story, after all,' she said.

'But it still might be true,' I insisted.

That afternoon I insisted on driving down to Dromore to see this place for myself, and I stood on a small hill looking out across the green fields of County Down, thinking that my ancestors had probably stood in that same spot and seen those same undulating hills, the Mournes, in the distance, and I thought of my brother and me in the bright sunshine of a December day before he died.

Later, we drove from Dromore towards Ballynahinch, turning towards Dromara. We drove around and around in the darkening afternoon, searching for a place called Drumaknockan. We drove up and down the same lane seven or eight times, with my mother saying that it was a waste of time, driving around the country like this, 'in the middle of bloody nowhere'. Eventually she just went silent and refused even to look at me. There were few people to ask directions of.

Eventually I stopped at a farmhouse and the farmer called for his wife and they both smiled when I asked for directions to Drumaknockan.

'Oh, there's no such place,' they said.

I looked closely at their faces, searching for a hint of some familial or cultural resemblance. The farmer called out for his mother and she came out slowly, leaning on a stick.

'There's a Drumaknockan Lane, if that's any good,' she said, and she gave me some complicated directions that reminded me of the old joke: *If I were looking for Drumaknockan Lane, then I wouldn't really start from here.* These folk had a vacant sort of smile, a little vulnerable, I thought. Not wily country people, like we imagined back in Ligoniel.

Eventually we found it. It was just a road sign, at the bottom of a windy hilly lane. I jumped excitedly out of the car and just stood there, goose bumps on my arms, and stared at the crows in the empty green fields, and studied the deep ruts in the earth and tried to visualize working the fields around here.

This was my home; I stood for ages, slightly teary-eyed.

When I got back to the car, my mother spoke for the first time in ages and said that she wanted to go home. 'There's nothing here,' she said. 'There's nothing but empty bloody fields. What have you been staring at?'

But I had found something that day, on one side of my family at least. I was elated and my mood seemed to annoy her. The next question for me, of course, was how long my family had been there. This was going to take a little more research, but it had been easy so far. I made a few jokes as we drove back to Belfast, mainly about how I was descended from landowners at least on my father's side. But my mother wasn't amused. 'Well, your da never had any bloody money,' she said, 'I'll tell you that for nothing. So it never did him any good.'

I returned to Manchester, but was keen to get back to Belfast to continue my research. Then one day in 1999 I got a phone call from one of my mother's friends telling me that my mother had had a fall in the house.

15

I arrived on a Friday morning at an Antrim Road nursing home that looked a little run-down and shabby. I got the directions to my mother's room and there she sat, small and vulnerable, the bathroom a few feet away, the television in the corner, a remote in her hand. She'd never had a remote before, and she flicked across the channels.

'I'm not staying here,' she said. 'I want to go home.'

The Social Services had suggested that she should come over to England and live with my family, but my mother had argued strongly against this.

'They're out all day at work. He's got this big dog with grey hairs on its face. My friends are all here.'

So they had arranged for her to go into the home – just for a few weeks, they said.

We talked about my family and my dog, the dog she loved to hate. She told me that she had read that the Japanese were bringing out mobile phones for cats and dogs and she suggested getting one for Louis, my dog.

'So that you can talk to him,' she said. 'I sometimes think that you'd rather talk to that animal than talk to me. I can't stand the way you kiss that creature.'

I asked my mother what it was like in this home and she just repeated that she didn't want to stay. 'And the staff are nearly all Taigs,' she whispered.

'But do you like them?' I asked.

'I don't trust Taigs,' she replied.

'But do you *like* them?' I asked again.

'They're all dead on,' she said and we both laughed. 'It's bloody daft, isn't it? I grew up with Taigs, I worked with them all my life – it's these bloody Troubles, they make you think stupid,' she said.

She talked about old times and about me and Bill when we'd been young. She always said that all she ever wanted was for us to be together. 'I remember coming over the Hightown one night, with your father and you and Bill in the car, and I was scared because it was dark but then I thought that we were a family all together and that if we went off the road and we died then we'd still be together. And then I realized that I wasn't scared any more.'

But I suppose at that very moment I realized that there was a corollary to all of this: that if we were not together my mother would feel even greater fear than everybody else. I felt terrible inside because here she was completely alone in that room. I tried to cheer her up by telling her that I had seen a sign saying that there was going to be a party that afternoon in the home. A Country and Western singer was coming in and I said that I would take her down to it.

'You're not going to leave me down there on my own, I hope,' she said.

I told her that I would stay with her.

'Have you had your run yet?' she enquired. 'I don't want you disappearing for one of those long runs of yours.'

I told her untruthfully that I had already had my run. She made a huffing sound. To distract her I told her that I had

162

seen a nice-looking man on the way in and she looked quite excited. I fetched her a small hand-mirror and she sat there doing her lipstick and brushing her hair forward, hair that was heavy with grey because she couldn't get near a sink to dye it. But she still looked well. I complimented her on her appearance.

'Well, your da always said that I was the best-looking girl in Ligoniel, and he had an eye for the girls so he knew what he was talking about.'

I got her Zimmer frame and lifted her into position on it. She always laughed when I manhandled her like that; it was a girly sort of laugh. We got through the door with difficulty.

A woman was coming out of the room opposite. She was much younger than my mother. Her face was heavily made up, the make-up covering deep cracks and lines. She could even have been quite young, it was hard to say; she looked like a very heavy drinker. The wall stopped her from falling. It could have been the drink or something altogether more grave.

'Is that your son?' the woman asked. 'Coming to take you out once a week, so that he can feel good about himself, so that he can feel like a big man.' The words were a little slurred; her backside was pushed outwards towards the wall for support. There was a fury in how she asked the question.

'Oh no,' said my mother, defending me. 'He doesn't live here. He's come all the way from England to take me out. He's a professor over there. He's very busy.'

'Too busy for his own mother?' the woman asked. Then, not hearing any immediate response, she said, 'Oh, have I put my foot in it?'

My mother nudged me with her elbow and I knew what

that meant: we had no time for people like this. My mother glared at her. The woman lurched from one wall to the opposite one in front of us and stood there as if she had been crucified, her arms out to her side, unable to move. She watched my mother, bent over the Zimmer frame, move towards the lift and the party downstairs.

We smiled at each other on the way down in the lift, and my mother said that it was terrible what drink did to people. In the party room old people sat in a circle like children, drinking out of paper cups filled with sherry or orangeade. I sat in the seat next to my mother. The woman to our left looked a little distressed.

'She's only forty-four,' said my mother. 'I don't know what the matter with her is. I think she's had a stroke.'

I noticed that this woman was gesturing with short batonic stabbing movements down towards her lap; she obviously couldn't speak. There was a wet patch between her legs that was spreading; her grey slacks were damp. I found myself staring down at the wet patch, and then looked away, feeling ashamed.

The much older man on the other side of her knocked the table to attract the attention of the woman serving the drinks, who went over to him.

'Do you want a drink?' she shouted. 'Orangeade or sherry?'

He knocked the table twice.

'I think that means orangeade,' she said and laughed to the rest of us. The woman in the light grey slacks was still gesturing. You could smell the urine now.

One of the care assistants came up to me. 'Do you want a wee sherry?' she asked.

'No, thank you,' I replied.

'What about a wee white wine?'

'No thank you.' I could see my mother looking over.

'I hope that you've been for your bloody run and that you're not going to spoil this party for me,' she said.

The woman beside us was still gesturing.

'It's a terrible pity,' said my mother, nodding towards her. 'And she hasn't even had her life yet.'

The Country and Western singer had started, and a very elderly man took one of the care assistants by the arm for a turn around the floor in this room reeking of piss both stale and fresh. I noticed that my mother was looking on in envy.

'He's a great mover for a man his age. A great mover.'

I went towards the toilet and glanced back and saw the look of undisguised envy in my mother's face. She was like a teenager at her first dance; she would have loved to have got up and danced that dull afternoon away, if it hadn't been for those ankles of her. I came back and sat with her for a few minutes and then told her that I had to go for my run.

'What did I tell you?' she said. 'I knew that you were lying – I can always tell. You and that bloody running.'

I told her that she would be all right and that she would enjoy herself. I left her trying to catch the eye of the grey-haired octogenarian who was moving so gracefully across the old carpet in front of so many admiring female eyes.

16

A few months later, after my mother had been back in her own house for a while, my Uncle Terence phoned me with bad news. He had already been in hospital for three weeks and was due to have a kidney removed. Then the operation was off. That was all I knew.

'Postponed or cancelled?' I asked, as if it was a football match. Then I heard the words down the phone: scan, tumour, growth. It had to be spelt out to me. Me with all that education, as he liked to say.

I went to see my uncle a week and a bit later in a hospital in Stoke-on-Trent; he had moved up to Stoke after my Aunt Agnes had died to be closer to his sister. I had a tape recorder in my carrier bag. My father had died suddenly after what was supposed to be routine surgery. My brother had died in that climbing accident. I didn't want to let my Uncle Terence go without the chance to talk to him – about our home in Northern Ireland, about the changes there, about the Peace, about my father, a man I could hardly remember, and how I was becoming the spitting image of him, at last. I wanted to tell him that I had just been appointed to be the Head of the Department of Psychology in Manchester, the oldest psychology department in the United Kingdom, and that all those years sitting studying at the card table in the front room in Legmore Street had paid off.

Terence's girlfriend, Marjorie, brought me to see him. My mother always referred to Marjorie as his girlfriend. It's a strange term, given that she was eighty-two and he was seventy-seven. Terence and Marjorie had been inseparable for twelve years or so, since my Aunt Agnes had died. My mother was always a little resentful of his second relationship.

'Look who's come to see you, Terry,' Marjorie said.

'So you got here, then,' he said, looking up at me. 'You've arrived at last.' He was always commenting on me being late for everything. 'What time do you call this?' he would say, after I had driven across England to see him. 'The Beatties are always late.'

My mother liked to tell the story of the day the whole street thought that we were dead in our beds because the woman who rapped us for work and school couldn't raise us.

'The Beatties would sleep all day,' Terence liked to say, 'if you let them.' He himself was an early riser.

He was sitting on a chair beside the bed, his bad leg up on a stool. He was my uncle but he was always more than that. Terence taught me to fish the streams coming off the mountains around Belfast, to fish with my hands. He would stand with his feet balanced on wet slimy stones in the middle of the bubbling brooks above Ligoniel and say, 'Get your hands in under the rocks and tickle them. Tickle their bellies. Trout love having their bellies tickled.'

167

I never caught anything that way, in contrast to Terence's own successful performance, even though I claimed to have had the odd tickle. However, I did once manage to pull a large dying trout out of a wide, weedy river one bright sunny afternoon in England and he photographed me holding it out in front of myself, the fish splayed across my open palms.

'Did you really catch that with your hands?' asked my brother, when he saw the photograph. 'Really?' My brother was a keen fly fisherman with hundreds of flies that he tied himself, and he didn't believe that you could catch brown trout like that in the middle of summer with your bare hands. He never really believed me even though he had the proof in front of him.

My uncle threw the dying fish back into a deep inlet in the river and it flopped about in the muddy brown water as if it couldn't right itself. But then its fins moved slowly and it disappeared.

'It wasn't dying,' said my uncle, not quite convincingly. 'Or it couldn't have swum away like that.'

But it didn't swim so much as sink.

Terence had boxed when he was younger, but it was only old people like Isaac the barber who could remember his boxing days. When I knew him he was always five stone or more overweight, always on a diet, and every Saturday night when he and my father got back from Paddy's at the bottom of the street my dog Spot and I would be invited to take him on. He would sit down in the chair by the window in our front room, heavy with drink, waiting for his supper, and beckon us towards him.

'Come on, get stuck in,' he would say.

The dog would jump up on the back of the chair and bite him in the neck and on the back through his jacket; I would club his large, heavy head with my fists. I can hear the noise of the dog now, that low growl from deep inside that would break up into a higher-pitched gnawing sound and then a yelp when Big Terry caught him with his hand.

'Give that dog a good skite,' my mother would say. 'It's getting carried away.'

The dog would only ever go for the big fella like that when he could smell the drink from him. So would I.

Not long after my father died, Terence left for England. So every summer I went to Chippenham to live with him and get some holiday work, and he would slap suntan cream on my back with those large manly hands to protect me from the torrid heat of Southern England as I set off for another day on a building site in Bath or Bristol. He had left Belfast because he always said that his promotion in the Civil Service was blocked because of his religion. He was a Fenian in the Belfast of the 1960s. The days of Unionist rule. He moved to England and got his promotion.

I came back to Belfast knowing from my holidays at Terence's place all about Ska and Reggae, and other things that never seemed to reach Belfast in those days. It was natural for me to go back across the water to study at university when the time came.

Terence sat on the chair by his bed in the hospital, full of a confused fury.

'I want to go home,' he said.

He asked me how the family was, but he seemed to be distracted, as if he couldn't wait for the answer. He had asked the doctor, who had given him his diagnosis of cancer, how long he had got left, but the doctor had told him that it was hard to say. All the talk was about who could look after him at home. All the talk was of the future. The illness was not mentioned.

The old man in the next bed called over to me. My Uncle Terence told me to ignore him. Terence told me that the old man was an attention-seeker. The old man said that he wanted me to fix his sleeve. I went over to him.

'Leave it,' shouted my uncle.

'Could you help an old soldier?' asked the other patient. I guided his arm into his sleeve and buttoned up his shirt. The nurse told me afterwards that the old man had had a stroke.

A confused-looking woman with a funeral-slow gait shuffled into the entrance of the ward. 'We call her the Rooster,' said Marjorie, 'because of the way she moves her head.' The Rooster peered in.

'Ignore her,' warned my uncle.

Her unsteady steps took her right into the ward. It was the male ward.

'She shouldn't be here,' said my uncle. 'Out, out, out,' he bellowed at her.

Her face showed not the slightest recognition of the message nor of its intensity, but she changed direction slowly like a large ship in the middle of the sea and walked away in a large unsteady arc.

'I need to get home,' said my uncle. 'This isn't the place for me.'

I tried talking about work and my promotion because he loved hearing all about what my education had got me, but he was far too distracted. He asked Marjorie and me to move the stool from below his bad foot and he shouted at us for doing it too slowly. He still had his personality.

By the time I returned ten days later, Terence had been moved to a side ward. I was now prepared for a repeat of the fury and the distraction of the previous visit. This image had intensified in my mind.

I found the main ward easily enough and glanced into all the other side wards with their doors open, hoping to catch a forewarning glimpse of what I might find when I got to his. On one bed there was a man lying in a foetal position. It seemed symbolic in a blatant sort of way – but who says that the meanings of life, the real meanings, have to be subtle? Entering and leaving the world, curled up and waiting for delivery into the next.

Terence lay back in bed, his head lolling to the side. His girlfriend was feeding him yogurt, which leaked out the side of his mouth. He already had the look of death about him. There was a void where his teeth once were. 'Terry O'Niell' read the misspelling above the bed. His left arm rested across his chest. A throw rug was folded above the pillow. A drainage bag clung on to the side of the bed. 'Single-patient use,' it read. A plant pot labelled *Rosanova* containing a couple of dying yellow flowers sat above the sink. There were a number of cards on shelves around the bed. I noticed that two of them were identical. My second cousin Ann and her husband sat quietly for a while by his bedside.

You could hear snippets of conversation coming from the corridor as patients' relatives made small talk with the nurses. 'He's a lot worse – his breathing, his colour.'

Terence lay there, looking like a ghost already. His toes, peeping out from below the blanket, resembled ripe figs. I noticed that his feet did not match. One was like greasy chicken, the other, bandaged and with an amputated toe, looked different. Diabetes, cataracts, a bad heart, cancer of the kidney, cancer of the lung. You name it, he had it.

My aunt and uncle had liked to enjoy themselves. That's what they always said. Smoking and drinking every night of their lives. They didn't have any children, so they always said that they might as well spend their money having fun in the only way they knew how in the Britain of the 1970s.

Terence's girlfriend said reluctantly that she had to go. She had been there all day and was exhausted. I stayed in the room, pleased to be alone with him. I could hear the hum of conversation from down the corridor, occasionally a child's voice. I sat watching his chest rise and fall rhythmically but shallowly. His nose hairs needed trimming.

A man passed slowly in a walking frame, then a nurse. She hardly dared smile at me in case it might start up a conversation that neither of us wanted. I did not want to ask her anything about my uncle, and she did not want to have to tell me anything. I have never seen a man go downhill so quickly; I didn't need any professional medical gloss on it.

My mind now was on all the private deaths in my family. It was Terence who had stopped me as a thirteen-year-old boy from going in to see my father in hospital the night he died in the Royal in Belfast. He had stopped me and my Aunt Agnes in the car park. I knew that it was bad news because he wouldn't look at me.

He was there in our front room in Legmore Street much later when we had the service for my brother who lay below a pile of loose stones on that Himalayan mountain. On that occasion he crept up to our back room for a sneaky cry. I caught him there with his back to the door, shielding his sorrow. He never liked showing any emotion in life, except perhaps anger and impatience. But they are manly emotions. Sometimes I think that I learned a lot from him – and not just about fishing and fighting with my bare hands.

*

I wanted to talk to Terence but I didn't want to listen to my own voice in that quiet room. I glanced into the blackened midwinter sky, hoping to see some distant stars. But all I could see were some lights glimmering through a fog out behind the hospital. I thought about what kind of man I had become and what my children will remember about me in thirty or forty years' time. A few frozen moments: a cross word here or there, a holiday perhaps. Not much.

Terence was peaceful, barely conscious, but I thought he was probably thirsty.

'Do you want some water?' I asked. There was no response.

'Do you want some water?' I repeated, much louder this time.

'Yes, please,' he replied. He seemed to be lapsing into unconsciousness but he remembered to say 'please'.

Marjorie had told me earlier that he would know that I was there. I held the plastic beaker to his mouth. He sucked at it like a child before it has got its first teeth.

I looked around the room, which I thought looked a little bare. Then I noticed what was missing. Terence had always been religious. He'd had all these little religious symbols when I was growing up. Symbols that I had to hide and shield from my friends back in North Belfast. But here there were none. He had been given the Last Rites the night before but now there was no sign of any Virgin Mary or Christ on the Cross or anything much. Just a bare hospital room with a few cards and some private possessions like slippers, but nothing more than that.

I had wanted to discuss the peace process with him, now that things were different. But I was too late. I was always too late for everything. That's what Terence always said.

We'd only discussed my father once, and that had been about a year previously. Terence said that I had shown no inclination to talk about my father after he'd died. He said that I just pulled the shutters down, I just closed the door.

And as for the Troubles, we never discussed them. Terence always said that one side was as bad as the other, and we left it at that. I don't think that I ever admitted to him that I knew that he was a Roman Catholic. We never spoke openly about it. I had been told a few years ago by my mother that Terence hadn't been allowed into the house of my Uncle Jack, who was a staunch Loyalist and had been married to my Aunt May, for nearly forty years. Forty fucking years. The years of fucking madness, I call them.

Only then did I realize why my Uncle Terence wasn't there that afternoon of my father's funeral, as we all sat around the wooden dining table. He wasn't allowed to be there because of his religion. He was my father's best friend.

The Rooster came to the door. She looked even more confused than the last time I had seen her.

'Everybody is going,' she said. 'I'd like to know where they're going.'

I didn't know whether this was profound or not.

She looked at Terence in the bed. 'I didn't know that he lived here,' she said. 'Maybe I will need it later on.'

But I didn't know what 'it' she was referring to. Just a confused old lady. She shuffled off slowly.

I asked Terence whether he wanted some more water.

'Not just at the moment,' he said. I learned to time my questions whenever there was a slight movement from him.

A nurse came in. 'Are you his son?' she asked.

'No, just a nephew,' I replied.

After she left, I felt myself smiling because I should have told her what I was thinking. 'He's a fucking Taig,' I said to myself, 'and I'm a fucking Prod from North Belfast. We're from fucking Murder Triangle; we kill each other over there. How the fuck could I be his son? Answer me that.'

My polite smile had turned to tears before I got to the end.

I spilt some water over Terence's pyjamas and he made a loud groaning sound as if I had scalded him with boiling water. This was my uncle. I asked him if he was in any pain.

He just said, 'It's starting,' but he didn't elaborate, no matter how much I pushed him.

I knew that he only had hours to live – I could sense it – but the staff nurse persuaded me that he was stable and that nothing would happen that night. So I left for the long drive home, and he died three hours later. I never did get the chance to talk to him. Always fucking late, that's my problem. He could have told you that. Always fucking late. It was the day before Christmas.

My mother came over to England for Christmas that year but she hardly talked about Terence except to say, 'They're all gone now – your father, your brother, my two sisters, now your Uncle Terry. I'm next.' She seemed almost happy about it. She couldn't make Terence's funeral because she was travelling back to Belfast that day. She wasn't inclined to change her travel plans, and Carol had to stay behind to take her to the airport. But on the morning of the funeral, my children Zoë, Ben and Sam trooped into her bedroom to show her how they looked in black. She sat up in bed and inspected them, the boys in their black suits and white shirts borrowed from me, Zoë in a black dress and a black jacket borrowed off her mother.

She was used to seeing them in jeans and trainers. 'They look lovely when they're dressed up,' she said. 'Like you and your brother when you were young. I have to say that there's something about Protestants when they're dressed up,' she went on. 'I hope you all look as nice at my funeral.'

We drove across the Pennines to a modern concrete-looking chapel in Stoke-on-Trent, the town to which Terence had retired to be near his sister after he had left the Civil Service. I had never been in a Roman Catholic church before, and I looked around at the few elderly women scattered among the pews. These ladies had braved the slippery pavements on that frosty morning to pay their last respects.

I watched my son Sam cross himself in front of the altar, because the woman in front of him had done it, and I laughed at this boy with pure Ulster Protestant blood who did not really know anything about the rituals and symbols of religious affiliation. When I had been his age, I used to watch out for people on the bus in Belfast crossing themselves as they passed the chapel at Ardoyne, just so that I could know who was one of us and who was one of them. But then I looked over at the coffin in front of the altar in that chapel, and thought of my Uncle Terence and remembered that he had blurred all of it anyway in my own mind. How could I have turned against somebody I didn't know just because they were the same religion as the Big Fella lying over there? Some of it didn't make much sense to me.

We moved on to the crematorium, Zoë and Ben mocking Sam gently in the back of the hearse for crossing himself, and then we watched the coffin slide behind the curtains. Nobody spoke.

I rang my mother that night and she asked me how the funeral had gone and I told her about Sam and how he had crossed himself.

'Oh, God love him,' she said.

I adored these old expressions that she used, the kinds of things that my age group never said. Things that would be lost, I suppose, within a generation.

I talked again about the night that Terence had died and I remembered that at one point in the hours before he had expired he had sat bolt upright, apparently full of surprise and shock. I had seen it in the films but I didn't know that it was based on anything real.

'He's gone,' said Ann's husband. He had been introduced to me as the husband of my second cousin, but not as a doctor, which he was. The doctor took Terence's pulse and then changed his mind. 'No, he's not gone yet.'

My mother listened attentively. I told her again that I was sorry that I had not been there at the end.

'It's just as well that you left,' she said. 'People behave very outrageously when they're dying.' 'Outrageously' – that was her word. 'They sent me out when your father was dying. They didn't want me to see it.'

And again she told me the story of my father playing with the ring on her finger as he lay there in that coma for a week, squeezing her hand when she asked him to but not able to speak himself. It was my main image of dying, even though I had not experienced it first-hand. The person, my daddy, trapped in this helpless body for seven days, unable to move, unable to communicate properly. It was like being buried alive. The story, which was meant to comfort me, had terrified me as a child and it still terrified me. It was what death meant to me.

I told my mother that I would have liked to have been there at the end for my Uncle Terence.

'And what about for me?' she said. 'You'll probably miss mine. You're always bloody late for everything.'

177

I told her not to be so silly and that she had a lot of life left in her.

Three months passed. My mother said that she was feeling a bit down.

'I'm fed up,' she said.

So that weekend I went over. She hadn't been that well, but there was nothing new in that and we went out to a different restaurant each night. She insisted on the Bellevue Arms on the first night. It represented something to her; it represented my wife's father and mother out every Saturday night, out enjoying themselves when she was stuck in the house on her own, with only what was in the glass for company. It represented the good life. I never liked it. Thick juicy steaks awash in their own juices, the liquid sloshing off the plate.

My mother was sick in the restaurant that night. She couldn't eat. I fetched her some paper handkerchiefs and watched the runny vomit gurgle out around the pink hankies, which she had stuffed in and around her mouth. There was a young family on the next table looking intently at her and then looking away and pretending that they couldn't hear her retching. The children played 'I-spy' to distract themselves.

I, for once, did not feel ashamed. I felt almost useful, and not paralysed by my normal social embarrassment when things go slightly wrong. She was bokeing. That was her word for the sounds she was making.

The next night we went down to Groomsport and I helped my mother out at the front door of the restaurant and left her standing in her Zimmer frame while I parked the car. But when I got out I could see her being helped up by two men. The wind had blown her over and she had hit her head. But she said that she was fine and she spent most of the night talking about the lovely fellas who had helped her up.

I left her on the Sunday night to get back to my work.

We talked on the phone and she said that she had had a lovely weekend, apart from that old sickness in her stomach. She couldn't stop bokeing.

This all seems like such a long time ago now. The Thursday morning after my mother's fall I was back home in my digs in Manchester when I got a phone call from my wife Carol in Sheffield.

My mother had had a stroke.

17

It is eight o'clock at night and I am watching the monitors to which my mother is attached. There are three of them, one above the other. The vital signs of life for all to see, for those sitting in judgement to watch. She lies there: her hair appears to be growing again now, her false teeth have been taken out, but you would not really notice. One eye is open; the other is closed. The massive stroke in the right side of her brain has meant that her eyelid on the left side cannot react to dust and light. It is closed. It looks as if she is watching me with her other eye – she is keeping an eye on me, even now. Her temperature is very high, so high that steam appears to be rising off her head. I touch it gingerly. Her forehead feels moist.

I had got the news that morning. I had heard the word 'stroke' and I had felt numb.

The female nurses do not make eye contact. I look at them, the way I always do. It is a look inherited from my mother. She was always used to admiring glances from strangers in the street, and as she got older she had to fish for that same admiration, that same level of interest, not with words but with sly looks. I think that I am the same sometimes, but the two scrubbed nurses never once look back, and I feel so very alone.

The doctor had told Carol and me earlier that he would not revive my mother if her heart stopped. He spoke in a matter-of-fact sort of way. The significance of what he'd said did not sink in at first and I almost forgot to ask why. Was she too old? Too ill? Too neurologically damaged? They had revived her once already when she'd been brought in, the doctor explained, but that was before the brain scans.

'Before we saw the extent of the damage,' he said. He looked me in the eye to see how I was taking it. He told me not to get my hopes up.

Muriel had found my mother that day. Muriel was her new best friend. All of her old friends except Sadie had died. My mother never minced her words. They had not 'moved on', nor had they 'passed on', nor were they 'no longer with her'. They had just died. Now there was Muriel.

My mother had kept her friends since schooldays, friends that had never moved away from Ligoniel, but I did not really know Muriel. She had appeared from nowhere a few years ago. A bit of a busybody, but very well meaning. My mother depended on her. She insisted that Muriel had lived in the neighbourhood for years, but in one of the better houses – that was why I did not know her. Muriel had found my mother that morning – Muriel with the impeccable hair and the busy-bee manner, active in the church, active in the Mothers' Union, active in the thrift shop. Active in my mother's house.

I would visit my mother and Muriel would be tidying up around her. My mother with her bandaged ankles up on the chair in front of her, unable to get up, unable to move with Muriel busying herself around the house. The previous weekend, my mother had put on some make-up for me.

'She wants to look her best for her son,' said Muriel. 'You shouldn't have done that,' said Muriel, 'Geoffrey will think that you are feeling well and you are not, Eileen, you are not well, at all. Your son should know.'

Muriel did not display any emotion that day. I had that glassy sort of numbness.

'Do you mind if I come in with you?' she asked Carol and me in the reception area of the hospital that day. 'It's not that I'm nosy. But I found her. She had an alarm that she kept round her neck,' Muriel continued. 'For emergency use only, just like the situation she found herself in. It got tangled around her neck. She was making these little noises when I found her. Ga, ga, ga, just like that.'

I glanced at Carol, who stared back in disbelief. Muriel did not seem to notice.

'Ga, ga, ga,' Muriel repeated without really looking at us. 'And', Muriel added, 'she had soiled the bed.' She made a facial expression to go with it. It was the expression of a woman with immaculate hair from a parlour house wrinkling her nose up at something disgusting – the state of my mother on the last day of her life.

My mother's heart rate is now going though the roof and her temperature is still rising. I pray to God for her recovery with that degree of intensity that only affects people at times like this. And then I remember the night before.

I had been driving from Sheffield to Manchester after midnight the previous night and as I was driving through Glossop a huge black dog had run out in front of my car. I had slammed on the brakes and the car behind had stopped abruptly too. The black dog looked in at me. It had no collar and it looked like a Rottweiler – it was that kind of size and build.

My car had stalled. I sat there for a moment. The dog walked onto the pavement. I started my car up again, and the dog ran beside the car. I watched it in my rear-view mirror as I accelerated away.

It was an experience sufficiently odd to mention when I got to Manchester. What was a dog like that doing out on its own at that time of night? I had been driving this route for six years and had never seen a dog out on its own before, let alone one like that.

But big black dogs signify death, don't they? I thought of that and I told myself not to get my hopes up. Not like I had done with my father, who had lain in a coma for a week: every day when I got home from school I would wait to hear some reassuring word that never came. The dog, out on its own, was a message from God.

But I tried one last time, despite this warning. If God let my mother get better I would look after her as I should have. I would give up work and tend her. There would be just her and me. That was the way she had always wanted it.

A male nurse brings in some blankets so that Carol can lie down. She goes and has a brief sleep. There are three other patients in intensive care. There is one woman who seems fine and smiles over at us a lot but never mentions my mother, and two other patients who are attached to all the tubes and instruments of modern medical aid and never move. At one point all the alarms attached to the male patient go off and the emergency team run to his assistance.

'One, two, three, clear!' And they shock him back to life.

183

But there will be no last-minute intervention here at our bed.

The male nurse, who talks quietly, closes my mother's other eye for her.

'That's better,' he says.

I want to nod as if I am in agreement but I can't. It is now my turn for a break. I go to the rest room and put the television on. There is a programme reviewing the latest porn releases. I watch two nude girls cavorting at Loch Ness.

I go back to my dying mother. Carol watches me to see how I am taking it. I can feel myself staring blankly.

My mother's minister arrives. We have never met. We shake hands, and he gets the Bible out. My mother often complained that he never really came to visit her, the way some earlier ministers had done when she had been a regular member of the congregation, when she could still walk.

I don't know whether to mention this, to turn my sorrow into anger. That is my style, my strategy for life itself. But I leave it aside as he prays – not, I notice, for my mother's recovery but for strength and help for the rest of us.

It is a long and distressing night. On a chair with no back, I am bent forward as if half in prayer, watching three sets of electronic data. I cannot let my thoughts move forward or back.

The male nurse assumes that I know little and carefully explains what each signal represents. I almost start to explain that I am a university professor and that my mother worked all those years in the mill to get me to university. Of course, I never believed that she did all that for me. I thought that it was my right to go off to university to leave her in Ewart's Mill or Ulster Plastics. That is how lucky I am. I just got what was coming to me.

The nurse tells me what to look out for on the monitors in front of me. I fall into the role that has been constructed for me.

'How high should the temperature be at this point?' I ask, as I watch the steam rise over her forehead.

'Not that high,' he responds. 'We must try to get her temperature down.'

I watch the temperature and the blood pressure and the heart rate rise and fall, one knocking against the other, changing and reconfiguring in front of me. Hour after hour, until you almost want something to happen.

I think of her fall in Groomsport and I blame myself for what happened.

Eventually, in the morning, I watch my mother's heart rate drop slowly until pauses start occurring in the beating of the heart. Then the pauses lengthen. I hold her hand.

'Can you see my brother?' I say. 'Bill is there waiting for you. Can you see Bill?'

I hope that she is entering a tunnel with light at the end. I am trying to reassure her. She always told me that my father could sense her presence until near the end. I want her to know that I am there and I am trying to tell her not to be frightened. But I am terrified of her dying, of her leaving me behind.

The pauses lengthen and lengthen until a flat line registers on the monitor in front of me, and I realize that my mother has gone.

I try to think of her words, I try to think of what she

would say. 'We're all going to die some time,' she would say. She was always very matter-of-fact about it. 'I'll be with your father and your brother again. It doesn't bother me. We will all meet up again. Don't you worry. It's only natural.'

She said that about everything – it's only natural. Why are men such selfish bastards? It's only natural. Why do people want to skive at work? It's only natural. And here she was – as she had long predicted – dying, although she had always said that I would never be there for her. She always said that I would be late.

But perhaps I was. Perhaps it was she who had waited for me. Perhaps she knew me that well.

18

The next morning Carol told me that she was going back to England to fetch our children for the funeral. I was angry and disappointed to be left alone in the house for the rest of the weekend, with my mother's slippers beside the table, her Zimmer frame waiting there at the top of the stairs, and the whiskey, half drunk and half watered, behind the bread bin. I knew that I would have to clear the house out. I walked around, looking at all the things that she had collected over a lifetime, knowing that I would have to go through it all item by item.

In a kitchen cupboard I found a manila envelope stuffed with articles that I had written, some of them academic papers – about pauses and phonation and cycles of semantic planning as speech is being conceptualized – and I wondered what my mother had made of these. The address was at the bottom: The Psychological Laboratory, University of Cambridge.

You could imagine her showing them to her friends. The words in the papers would have meant little, except perhaps for the address. 'Oh, Cambridge – he's awfully clever, your Geoffrey.' One article was about Carol losing her arm in the accident; it was the first piece I ever wrote that was not academic. It was why I had become a writer.

She had kept them all safe; I always thought that she threw everything out.

My mother had collected a lot of cheap ornaments and photo frames over the years. My children bought her photo frames with white shells on a sea-blue background or in plastic 'mahogany' – those folded out like a book – as presents at Christmas or for birthdays. In the kitchen there was an exotic-looking brass tea caddy sitting on top of a record player that had not worked since I was a boy. It had old records from the 1960s piled up on the turntable: Manfred Mann, the Kinks, Roy Orbison. The record player was used as a cabinet because it had legs and a wooden casing around it. The tea caddy looked as if it was from the Middle East, but it was actually from Debenhams. I had bought it for her as a present, ostensibly from Turkey. No doubt she had shown it proudly to her friends.

'All the way from the kasbah,' she would have said. 'He carried that all the way home to Belfast for me.'

I thought it was a harmless deception. But perhaps in years to come my descendants will turn my house upside down, searching for the tea caddy from Turkey. They will have seen it sitting there in the back room and they will have heard the story.

The previous weekend, I had gone to Boots and bought my mother some Complan because she could not eat anything solid. The box lay in the cupboard, still full except for one sachet that we had shared together. We'd spent ages trying to remember the name of the drink that I had taken in my early teens after I had started running. It was just a food supplement but I thought it would turn me into some sort of superman.

I moved around the house from room to room, peering into the wardrobes and my mother's cubbyholes, just looking at the amount of stuff. That's what she would have called it – 'stuff'. I realized that nearly all her personal belongings would either have to be given away or thrown out. There was a cubbyhole packed with her clothes in the front bedroom, the bedroom that I used when I stayed with her. I burrowed into these garments to smell her old perfume and I noticed that this enclosed space was much deeper than I had ever imagined. She could never have got in there in the last few years of her life, and perhaps not even before – she was never that nimble. I pushed past the shoes and the dresses and the coats and there at the back was an old suitcase. It had been probably been pushed in there by the workmen when she had first moved to the new house. The lock didn't work so I pulled it open. It was crammed full.

There lay my old school textbooks, and my physics lab books, Bill's school cap and his reports from Everton Secondary School, details of a pantomime at St Mark's with Bill in the line-up and a yellowed bit of parchment lying at the bottom: my grandfather's discharge papers from the army. All the things that I thought had been bulldozed into the debris back at the old house. I tried to imagine Bill in his cap on his first day at Everton, but that image could not be evoked no matter how hard I tried. Also in the case was a copy of *The Adventures of Tom Sawyer*, with that cover where the beautiful blond Tom bites the apple and the little black boy in the group has these big white eyes and looks like he's wearing red lipstick. Two seagulls hovered on the spine, which used to peek out of the bookshelf in the back room in Legmore Street. There too lay the *First Latin Composition Book*, from form IVA, with some handwritten pages inside in what must have been my own neat writing: 'He is afraid to escape – *timet effugere*'; 'I hope to see you – *spero me te visurum esse*'. That old musty smell of damp from the old house had impregnated each and every page. It was like being back there for a moment.

There were details of my grandfather's army record on that discharge paper – he did twelve years in the army, nine years, two hundred and ninety-four days' service abroad, serving in the Royal Inniskilling Fusiliers. I discovered that he had joined up at eighteen in 1893 and had been discharged in 1905 in Londonderry. He got the India Medal in 1895, with two clasps, and the Queen's South Africa Medal, with three clasps, and a Second Class Certificate of Education. I didn't know any of this. His trade was given as a rougher in the linen industry. 'His conduct and character while with the Colours have been according to the Records: Indifferent.'

It was, regardless of his indifferent conduct, a connection with our Protestant heritage; William of Orange had formed the Royal Inniskilling Fusiliers in 1689. The 27th Regiment got their first 'badge' for the defence of what was then called Inniskilling (now Enniskillen) in 1691. According to Richards's classic text *Her Majesty's Army*: 'Throughout the Irish wars which followed the accession to the throne of William III, from the passage of the Boyne to the fall of Limerick, the 27th fought gallantly for the new order of things.'

My grandfather George would have known all about their glorious history as he sang the Sash, which commemorated their great victories. The Inniskillings fought at Culloden, they fought at Brooklyn, White Plains

190

and Georgetown in the American War of Independence, and they fought under Wellington at Waterloo. According to Richards, they 'joined Wellington's army on June 16th, marching through Brussels without halting, and arriving on the field of Waterloo on the 18th. It was well for the gallant Inniskillings that they made that forced march, for no regiment gained greater honour in that tremendous conflict. They were in Lambert's Brigade, the Sixth, and at one time we are told, "So heavy was the fire on the 27th Regiment that in a few minutes it was reduced to a mere cluster, surrounded by a bank of the slain."'

My mother had always said that her father was a big man: 'Oh, much taller than you or your father,' she liked to say. But this bit of yellowed paper informed me that he was five foot eight with a dark complexion, brown eyes, black hair and with a mole close to his right nipple. I wanted to show her my find. I needed to tell her about it. And at the bottom of the case was a bronze-coloured broken-clasped badge with a number of capital letters in the shape of an arc. The letters spelt out 'INNISKILLING'.

I went downstairs and put on the TV, the TV that my mother had bought second-hand off old Joe, and which had never worked properly since she had got it. I sat there, with that yellow parchment from the War Office in my hand and the little badge, listening to the buses shuddering past the door, racing up the Ligoniel Road the way that they always did, and I started to weep like a wee child, knowing that the whole street could probably hear the racket from this house with its walls as thin as fucking paper.

The next day I went around knocking on the doors of my mother's old friends, giving away some of her clothes. She and I had been up to Makro earlier that week and she had got some new gear; it had not been worn, and her friends who had known her all her life accepted it gratefully.

'It's still got the label on,' said Vera, one of her neighbours.

I was pleased that they were taking the garments. My mother had got a new wardrobe of clothes when her friend Lena had died. She could hardly fit them into her own wardrobe.

I suppose that morning I felt that I was celebrating some aspect of working-class life, the customs of a group who do not seem too sentimental when it comes to material things like clothes or ornaments after their owners have died. My mother would have wanted me to give them away like this.

There was just one thing that she wanted me to keep: her gold locket with flowers on the front and small hazy photos of Bill and myself at my wedding, torn down to size, pushed into each half. That was our family heirloom. That was what we would pass on; it was always intended for my daughter Zoë. My mother's ornaments went to the Mothers' Union thrift shop up at St Mark's.

I just kept back the clothes that she was to be buried in because she was always a great one for the style; I selected something nice.

And as for the funeral itself, my mother had always told me that she never wanted to be carried by me in case I dropped her.

'You can be very careless,' she always liked to say. 'You've always been a very careless boy.'

But I never told anyone about her wish.

We stood outside St Mark's, waiting for the coffin. There was to be just the one lift, down to the front gate. My eldest son Ben and I linked arms, with George, my cousin, and

Tom, Jacqueline's husband, standing behind. My mother would have been proud of how the four of us looked in our black suits and our white shirts. We Ulster Protestants always look good when we are burying our own.

When we lifted her out at Roselawn there was a slight decline, which I had never really noticed before, down to my father's grave. Our steps quickened on the wet grass, and Ben and I gripped each other hard to keep the coffin steady, but for a moment I was sure that we were going to drop her. And as we laid her to rest, I thought to myself that she had been right about most things, when it came down to it.

Let's face it: she was a very shrewd woman.

19

Three months later, in July 2000, I decided to go back home for the Twelfth Week, the annual Protestant celebrations commemorating King William of Orange's victory at the Battle of the Boyne. I hadn't been to them since I was a child. My mother had come over to Sheffield every July for her annual holiday for years; we used to go on day trips, 'a day here and a day there', as we'd called it when we were kids. We used to have a day here and a day there in the Peak District, which was not much of a holiday really, and we could go only when I wasn't busy. But there was nothing keeping me in Sheffield that July, and I felt the need to go home.

Ulster was at a virtual standstill because of the government's refusal to allow the Orangemen to march their traditional route at Drumcree Church in Portadown. The Orange Order had called for peaceful protests, but the protests had got out of hand.

I drove to Bangor. The pull was towards North Belfast – it was always going to be like that, like the tug of a great invisible magnet. But by forcing myself to ignore the impulse and heading towards the motorway and the other destination from the international airport at half-past seven in the morning, I found myself on the road to Bangor. And to my childhood: summer holidays in Pac-a-macs, driving rain, warm smells, fish suppers and hard sweet rock that nearly broke your teeth and condemned me to a lifetime of fillings in my molars. Of course, my mother had remembered it differently.

'The best time of my life,' she always said, 'was down in Bangor when you children were young. There was your dad and myself and you and Bill on the Twelfth Week down by Pickie Pool. None of us could swim, so we all just paddled in the water and walked along Queen's Parade in the sun, watching the boys in the rowing boats and we listened to the open-air service on a Sunday morning. "Abide with Me". I can hear it now.'

I had always liked her talking about those days; I liked how it changed her face. The images flickered across her eyes, and for those moments she always seemed younger.

I found a room on Queen's Parade itself, in a guest house that overlooked the sea. I was in the back bedroom, though, with a view of nothing in particular, which seemed appropriate. Just a roof and some windows with curtains that stayed closed, although it wasn't clear whether there was anyone behind them.

But this, I suppose, would have been my mother's dream: a hotel – and she would have called it that – right on the seafront. She always talked about Bill and me drinking with her in a bar in Groomsport, when I had been supposed to be somewhere else. A few bottles in the middle of the afternoon with that warm smell of beer that had soaked into the carpet. Just the three of us, what was left of the family together, the way it should be.

An elderly woman sat in the next garden along, watching me drag my case up the short flight of steps. She had thin legs that seemed to be knitted together – as if she might need the toilet. Her legs drew attention to themselves like those of a pre-pubescent girl. You didn't want to look, but you couldn't stop yourself. She was getting a packet of cigarettes out of a tattered black bag and had a thin smoker's face.

'You must be a late arrival,' she shouted.

She left a gap for me to say something, but I just made a sort of 'Hmmmmm' sound.

'We're just going,' she shouted. But she seemed to be on her own.

I lifted my heavy case up the remaining steps and then paused. The woman was lighting her cigarette and sitting in the cool morning air, looking out towards the white shiny boats in the new marina. The seaside. I breathed deeply through my nostrils and noticed that every fourth breath or so you could smell the sea air. The other three breaths you couldn't. The atmosphere just smelt of modern life, but not necessarily of petrol or fumes. It was more anonymous than that.

'Did you have a nice holiday?' I asked.

'Oh, it was lovely,' she said. 'Lovely.'

She sounded like my mother. I was dreading that. Elderly Belfast women were going to sound like her – the Protestant ones, anyway. Part of me wanted to hear the voice. I had been dialling my mother's old number just for that sense of anticipation of hearing her. Just to get ready to speak to her. I never knew what to expect when I rang her, I could never predict what kind of mood she would be in. If she were in a bad mood, I would sense it immediately, in the very timing of that first pause before she answered. That pause, especially if it opened up and started lengthening, told you everything.

Drink changed everything too. There were dark, black moods fuelled by drink. She would always justify the bad moods.

'Is it any bloody wonder?' she would say. 'You don't know what it's like, living alone. But you may do, one day.'

There was no public face, no mask. She told you what she thought.

Anticipation, that's the right word for it. Never knowing what was going to happen in those first few microseconds at the other end of the phone. So I still rang that pattern of numbers, her telephone number, at the end of the day at work, at my normal time. That mysterious configuration of hand movements made me feel strange. A muscle memory, that's what the advertisement about Andy Cole, the Manchester United striker, was calling it at the time. That sequence of moves across the array of numbers, those muscle movements, made me almost freeze. Then I would try to hang up just before the line went dead.

The old woman sucked in the smoke from her untipped cigarette. She had thin cheeks, hollow with age and smoking.

'I love Bangor,' she said. 'I always have done.'

I was dreading her saying 'since when the children were young'. She was sounding even more like my mother, with that slight drawl on the vowel in the middle of the word 'love'. As if this drab, grey place with its high-fronted houses overlooking a choppy Belfast lough was in some way special. It was just plain buildings in a dullish light, as if there was no real light and no foreground and no background. There was no depth and no perspective. But every fourth breath reminded me of where I was, back in the sun in Pickie Pool with a family paddling together, and a sense of belonging.

'What's the weather been like?' I asked.

'Not too bad,' she said. 'It hasn't rained every day.'

She stressed the word 'every', and particularly the first syllable. It was that sort of getting-by. It hinted back to the years of the Second World War seen from afar, with men in uniform walking along with smiling girls who were showing some leg in their stockings, just a hint of soft, white thigh, the war years captured in sepia prints curling at the edges, and my mother's stories about the great days with the Yanks. Young men and women living with whatever optimism they could muster.

My mother liked to talk about her years as an air-raid warden. There had been a shelter at the top of our street, and then the Big Yanks arrived in Belfast, with their big talk about life in Wisconsin or upstate New York, and their pockets full of candy bars and stockings – and money, although the money was always implicit rather than explicit. But none of her stories ever involved her with any of those Big Yanks. It was always somebody else.

Her best friend fell for a Big Yank, and Agnes also fell for one before she fell – and 'fell' was always the important word here – for Big Terry, who was, of course, a Roman Catholic. Agnes would have had to fall for a Roman Catholic. There could be no other explanation.

But my mother was curiously missing from all her own stories, although my father popped up sometimes in her wartime escapades, driving a Rolls-Royce that didn't belong to him. He was a chauffeur for Harry Ferguson. That was the story, but I never thought to ask whether he was a chauffeur for the company or for the man himself, the man behind Ferguson tractors.

My father got to park the car at the end of the day and sometimes he took a detour up to the mill village of Ligoniel to see a girl with black hair and slim tanned legs and friends who were all being chased by Big Yanks.

The elderly woman sat there at the table in the cold morning air, puffing her cigarette and looking out to sea. 'Pickie Pool is just over there', she said. 'If you get a chance you must go and pay a wee visit.'

I nodded.

'Where have you come from?' she asked.

'Manchester,' I replied.

'Oh, you're a Mancunian.'

Hardly, I wanted to say. I have skinned my shins too many times on the concrete round Pickie Pool to be a Mancunian. There are black and white photographs of me being pushed in my pram in the wind and the rain up and down Queens Parade. You can see my big round face – my mother called it my 'moon face' – sticking out of the pram and with these same houses in the background. I belong here.

'I'm not really a Mancunian,' I said.

'Oh,' she replied.

'I'm from Belfast.'

'Oh, you've lost your accent, then,' she said. 'You sound all English.'

The proprietor of the guest house was English and a man. My mother would have been surprised, on both counts. The house was spotless, freshly painted and with plastic flowers in bowls, and the landlord wore a permanent smile. It turned out that he had previously been a manager for B&Q somewhere in England. He showed me to my room and he explained how the television worked, as if I might be an imbecile.

'Oh, and by the way, what time does Pickie Pool open?' I asked.

'Oh, you know about Pickie Pool then?' he said.

'I know Pickie Pool all right,' I said and I felt myself fill up just for a second so that I had to wipe the corner of one eye in a casual way.

'They have big white plastic swans there now, you know,' he said, 'and a miniature railway. You'll hardly recognize it. It's not a paddling pool any more, it's a fun park.' I think that he was trying to reassure me.

'A fun park? That sounds really good,' I said without any conviction in my voice. I retired to my room and decided to go for a run.

I ran along the seafront to Ballyholme, past grey slate rocks and a warning not to eat the shellfish, past a girl with a tanned pretty face who threw a shy, sly smile through a thick curtain of dark shiny hair, past a small mountain of cigarette butts in a corner of a car park, past Ballyholme Yacht Club and the pop-pop-popping of tennis balls, past a girlie mag half ripped and discarded just opposite the King's Fellowship, which had a sign outside that read 'God Keeps His Word'. A reassurance or a warning? I wasn't sure which as I jogged along in that small personal bubble that excludes all others. The sweat in my eyes stung like sharp tears. I was taking it all in, seeing everything and yet part of nothing.

I sat at breakfast the next morning, watching the boats rock this way and that in the marina. It was another greyish day. There was an old woman at the next table, waiting for her breakfast. I had watched her peep out from behind her door, waiting until the coast was clear. She was older than my mother. I had started hating seeing women who were still mobile, who could still get about on their own, and who were nevertheless older than my mother.

This was a woman of some independence; she had somehow managed to get to Bangor all on her own. My mother had for years longed to have a chum – it was another of her words – a chum to go away with and this old lady had done it by herself. But she was hard of hearing.

'Cornflakes and then prunes,' she said to the young waitress, the daughter of the smiling owner.

The young waitress said, 'What?'

'Prunes, please. PRUNES.' The old lady went back to focusing on the white empty plate in front of her, a sparkling plate, as if she was trying to work out how you could get a plate so clean. She remembered those Twelfth Weeks by Pickie Pool, I could tell. That's why she was here too. She stood by her door waiting for the toilet in the corridor to be free in the afternoons. It took her a while to get there, leaning on her stick.

The young waitress presented her with the dinner menu even though we were having breakfast. The old lady was still on her prunes.

'What do you want for dinner?' the waitress asked loudly. So loudly that even the couple who were deeply into themselves looked over.

'Can I order later?' the old woman asked.

'I'll go and see,' said the young waitress. She returned almost immediately. 'No, you have to order now.'

'I'll have fish, then.'

'Cod and chips and peas?'

'Just fish, please.'

'At five o'clock.'

'What?'

'At FIVE o'clock.'

'That's awfully early.'

'That's the time for dinner.'

'All right.'

The old lady finished her prunes, drained her cup of tea and looked out at the boats on the choppy grey waves. There was a strong wind that morning and the white plastic chairs in the front garden were huddled against the front wall. The sun was shining, but it was bitterly cold for mid-July.

The other guests made their plans for the day, plans which would involve staying inside cars and watching grey waves or hypnotically rocking boats, leaving just the two of us, me and her, in this place. We would have to talk, even though she was hard of hearing.

I smiled across at her, the way my mother would have done if it had been an elderly man sitting over there on his own. I caught her eye. She smiled at me and I looked down at the tablecloth demurely. She opened the conversation.

'It's always nice in Bangor,' she said. 'We came here every year, my Robert and I when the children were young. Ward Park, Ballyholme, Ballywalter, Groomsport, Donaghadee . . .'

I didn't really want her to continue. I knew the rest, so I sat in silence, just nodding but not enough to encourage her to continue.

She looked out at the waves again, as if to say that here was a young man who didn't want to be bothered with the reminiscences of an old woman near the end of her life. I watched her get up. She was shaking slightly, and she slowly and unsteadily made her way back to her room on the first floor. I followed her upstairs. It took an age. She was too bent by age to glance around.

The door closed behind her.

Even her memories were fading. That was why she was there. To remember, before she forgot forever. The sights, the sounds, the smells, the solitary squawk of a gull, the

202

tangy taste of salt in the air, the rain dripping from a plastic hood onto her lower lip, the outline of the houses at dusk, the one chimney pot that stood out from the rest, the sweep of the bay in the early-morning light, to bring Robert in his sports jacket and his lovely grey trousers, the ones that he wore every holiday, back down that road over there.

Just one last time.

I made my way into the centre of Bangor that afternoon and watched them getting out of a small Vauxhall saloon. There were five of them, crammed into this one small car; they all had thick necks whose rolls of fat were accentuated by their close-cropped hair. They wore casual shirts with Orange Order sashes over them. They seemed in a hurry. It was twenty past four and the Orangemen had called for the peaceful protests to begin at four o' clock precisely. They were obviously late.

They walked off briskly. The fifth stayed behind for a few seconds to lock the car and then he ran after his comrades. His love handles and his loop of cloth bobbed up and down as he ran. His burgundy shirt and his orange sash clashed horribly.

All the shops were already closed, as well as all the cafés and restaurants. I had lunch in a Kentucky Fried Chicken outlet, the only place left open. I asked the teenager behind the counter why they were still open.

He took my question as a challenge and told me in a defensive sort of way that KFC were not allowed to close. Colonel Saunders, or whoever is in charge, apparently knows or cares little about the politics of Northern Ireland.

I was starting to resign myself to eating dinner too that night in KFC, scanning the menu to try to work out a balanced diet in a land where no shops apart from fried-chicken places were staying open when the only other customers, a group of huddled teenagers, made their way outside and sprayed the window with a bottle of fizzy Coke.

'Fucking cunts,' one shouted loudly through the window. 'No fucking surrender. Close the fucking joint, or else.'

The young man behind the counter looked nervous. 'I only work here,' he said to me.

I made him promise to stay open that night.

'I could go on the sick,' he said. 'I *feel* a bit sick, to be honest. I wouldn't be lying.'

The streets, busy that morning, had cleared by now. They were deserted. I made my way up the road and then I saw them all. They had come from nowhere to mill around at the top of the street. Union Jacks, the Red Hands of Ulster and banners about apartheid flapped in the cold breeze. The Protestants were the victims now. Forget all that stuff about a Protestant land for a Protestant people, it was they who were being discriminated against. They positioned themselves across all the roads on the big roundabout just as you come into Bangor. And there they stood. Great lumps of men. Just chatting away.

'Like women,' my mother would have said if she had been there. 'Gossiping just like old women.'

There was a small human barricade on the road I was on. Five children who sat cross-legged across the road blocked the road up from the seafront. Their ages ranged from perhaps four to seven. The four-year-old was wearing National Health glasses – I thought that they had been phased out – a pink sweater and pigtails. Their father stood behind them; at least, I assume that he was their father.

Suddenly I heard a noise of a car engine roaring away. I

could see the driver of the car: a baseball cap back to front, young fleshy cheeks, hair shaved up the sides, an earring. I watched this boy racer speed towards the family group. He was a lump as well, like the men behind the child barricade. A shaven-headed lump wearing an earring. He drove a Peugeot 206, a real speed machine, and he was putting his foot down.

Neither the children nor the father standing behind them budged. The Peugeot driver was heading straight for them. I probably averted my eyes, just for a second, because the next thing I heard was the screeching of burning rubber tyres as the car accelerated up a street to the left, just a few yards in front of the barricade.

It had been a test of resolve. But nobody made any comment.

'No surrender,' it said on one of the banners fluttering in the chill wind. 'No fucking surrender,' said the tallest of the youths, the Coke sprayer from the KFC, right into my ear as they passed me, a man standing there in Bangor on his own, just watching what was going on, not part of anything. A man who clearly didn't belong, probably with an expression of mild distaste on his face. I think that the youth might have been trying to provoke me. They stopped a few feet away from me.

'Did you see that cunt in the car?' one said. 'Does anybody know that fucker's name or where he lives?' Young men acting big in front of a posse of spotty girls.

I looked around me. The roundabout was just by the entrance to Ward Park. My father and I had gone there to feed the ducks the week before he'd died. I have a photograph of myself in a Russian hat, my arm in a sling because I'd broken it at judo, taken just up there. I wondered what my father would have made of all of it, him being a Shankill Road man and all that.

'We are the victims,' read another of the banners. I laughed quietly to myself at this gaudy sea of orange and red, white and blue, peopled with fat gossipy men draped in bits of shiny cloth.

'We are all fucking victims, do you know that?' I said to the tallest youth, the one who had sprayed the KFC window.

He looked at me, a little surprised, as if I shouldn't have been in a position to speak. 'Too fucking right,' he said after a short pause. 'Too fucking right.'

His friends all cheered in a non-comprehending sort of way and looked at me as if they were waiting for me to cheer as well. They had heard the inclusive 'we', perhaps with a bit too much emphasis on that very first word, and that was quite enough for them – that day, at least.

Somebody patted me on the back. I smiled. 'I thought that you might be a newspaperman,' the tall youth said. 'And they're all fucking Taigs so we were a bit worried there for a minute.'

I reassured them that I wasn't from any newspaper.

'Where are you from, then, fella?' another youth asked.

'North Belfast,' I replied. 'The turn-of-the-road.'

'The fucking turn-of-the-road? The Upper Crumlin Road just before it turns into that Fenian hole Ligoniel?' he said. 'It's fucking wild up there – you must know some really hard men.' And he went on to recite a list of names from the headlines, a series of Protestant icons, some alive, some dead.

'I know them all,' I said. 'Or I did. I grew up with Tonto Watt and Den Eccles.'

206

'What about Lenny Murphy and the Shankill Butchers?' one asked.

'I probably met them, I don't remember,' I said.

'Why are you speaking all English, then?' asked the Coke sprayer, who was starting to take a lot more interest in me.

'I'm kind of in disguise if you know what I mean,' I said. 'It's a sort of deep cover. Do you know what that means?'

They all nodded meaningfully. 'Are you on the run?' said the Coke sprayer.

'I am indeed,' I replied. 'I am well and truly on the fucking run.' I said it with such emotion that they knew it was true. And they also could sense that they should not push it any further.

'Best of luck,' said the Coke sprayer as they left me.

'Take care, mate,' said his friends, and they all patted me on the back, every one of them in turn before they went, as if they were touching some lucky mascot. The Coke sprayer waved at me for good measure.

And I waved back.

20

The next day I drove up the Shankill to my mother's home. The road shimmered with new flags and bunting, which made it seem alive. There were some new murals on the gable walls and fresh banners stretched across the road. UFF, 'Simply the Best', UVF. Groups of teenagers and much younger boys were congregating on every street corner, just hanging about and waiting. Men in designer sweatshirts – Calvin Klein, Kickers, Ralph Lauren – watched any strange car like mine. The swagger was back in their walk. Hard men were back on the streets.

One of them gave me the look, the look that said it all. For a while I thought that look had gone out of fashion, but it had come back. The defenders of Ulster had a job to do once more, Ulster was under attack once more because the government had banned the Orange Lodge from marching down the Garvaghy Road in Drumcree.

I drove aimlessly around North Belfast for a while; I wasn't quite sure where to go without a home there any more. Then I drove slowly back to the city centre down the Crumlin, which seemed almost lifeless in comparison with the Shankill, down past the funeral directors' where my mother had lain weeks previously.

Town was closing early like in the bad old days. I went to a coffee shop and ate date and walnut cake off a bright green plate, with a double espresso to accompany it. It was one of the newer types of café whose opening in Belfast seemed to signal the sharp turn to normality that came with the ceasefire. But I was the last customer in there.

The waitress came over and told me that unfortunately they were having to close at four p.m. that day. I looked out and I could see that the shutters of the shops all around were already coming down.

'We want to get home safely,' she said. She advised me to go home. I told her that I had come over to Belfast for a visit.

'You decided to come over this week?' she asked. 'You decided to come over in the Twelfth Week?' She shook her head. 'It's not the best time to come over,' she said, and I noticed that smile of hers. She didn't seem to recognize my accent and she just assumed that I was there on holiday. 'Have you ever been down south?' she asked helpfully. 'It's nicer down there. Or there's Galway. It's a five-hour drive. But it's a lot more peaceful than around here. There's more of a holiday atmosphere down there. It's a lot more relaxed.'

It was nearly half-four on the Friday afternoon and I was just sitting without apparently a care in the world. She seemed to find this a little disconcerting. The waitress didn't realize that I had nowhere to go.

'Everywhere is closing,' she said. 'The shops, the roads, even the motorway. You should really be on your way, you know.' She told me again to go south of the border, to another country.

I told her that I intended to go to North Belfast and then to Portadown.

'I hope you like walking,' she said as she locked the door behind me.

I drove back up to North Belfast in a kind of directionless way as if I really wanted to go somewhere but couldn't – which I suppose made sense. The closer I got to the turn-of-the-road the more people I saw. I noticed that the tarmac at the turn-of-the-road was melted in a number of places. This indicated where burning cars had sat. The crash barrier from the library had been hauled out of its concrete base and pulled across the road and then back onto the pavement where it now stood. A burned-out car and bus sat just up from it by the top gate of the park, still in the middle of the road. The Catholic enclave at the top of Ligoniel was locked in.

There were gangs of children on the street corner milling about, looking a little excited. A child of about four walked towards the shops, whistling 'The Sash'. Two young girls, one about seven, one perhaps a year or so older, were looking after their baby sister in a pushchair outside the pub. A boy of about ten with a catapult dangling from his hand stood outside the sweetshop and was calling over to the two girls.

'I know you two, don't I?' he shouted. 'You can hang about over here with me if you fancy it. Bring your wee child if you like, I don't mind.'

A Red Hand of Ulster flag flew outside my mother's old house. A Loyalist family had obviously moved in. I wanted to see their faces, I wanted to go up to the door and rap it to see if I recognized them, to see if my mother would have approved, but I couldn't. They might be new to the area. I sat outside in my car reading the paper, glancing towards the window, hoping for a glimpse.

The paper told me that British troops were patrolling the

streets for the first time in two years. There was gridlock all over the city. There had been one hundred and five petrol-bomb incidents, and one hundred and nine attacks on the security forces in the past week. I saw a photograph in the *Irish News* of somebody called Samantha Brooks. I didn't recognize the name, but she was a Protestant from around here and the photo showed her sitting in what remained of her home just opposite my mother's house. Her house had been attacked because she had shacked up with a Taig.

I got out of the car and walked down to the corner past the house that had been demolished by the lorry. But I didn't see anybody that I knew so I got back into my car and just drove around instead, like somebody who didn't belong.

A small group of fourteen-year-olds watched me carefully as I pulled into the red, white and blue-painted kerb to make some notes. One tapped on the window.

'Are you a journalist?' he asked. 'Because if you are, you can fucking well fuck off. You lot always slag off the Protestants. You're all Fenian-lovers.'

I smiled at him, but he turned his back. I put the notebook away and sat motionless. It felt strange because I could not, in full view of them all, walk straight into my mother's house. It had almost stopped feeling like home. I just sat there for a while, looking out, not saying anything. Then I drove all the way back to Bangor and stopped on the front and watched the seagulls, with their wide, dirty, matted wings, as they swooped and tore at a greasy chip supper in the middle of the road. I drove through them and they scattered in all directions.

The next day I decided to go to the stand-off at Drumcree, the proximal cause of all this unease. It was early evening on the night before the proposed big march there. Some were saying that it was the quiet before the storm, but nobody was quite sure.

I drove to Portadown and then asked for directions. I got all sorts of conflicting advice about how to get to Drumcree, so conflicting indeed that it seemed almost deliberate. But eventually I found myself driving out of Portadown in the right direction and noticed that I was at the bottom of the Garvaghy Road, its tricolours flying defiantly, signalling its Republican status: the road that the Orangemen were banned from walking along.

But the RUC at the roadblocks seemed relaxed enough. Chatty, even. So I simply headed for the church spire on the hill and parked behind a row of burger and ice-cream vans.

Saturday was quiet, but the week as a whole had not been. The melted tarmac and the charred and twisted debris on and at the sides of the roads were testimony to the earlier unrest. There was a pervasive air of excitement.

There had been numerous burnings and hijackings. One unfortunate Loyalist in Belfast had tried to hijack an unmarked car with three plain-clothes RUC officers in it. He said that he'd thought that it was a taxi and that he wasn't so much attempting to hijack the vehicle concerned as trying to flag it down vigorously.

I had heard Martin McGuinness on Radio Ulster on my way to Drumcree describe the event as 'the last kick of Loyalism'. But the bunting and the flags and the swagger in the Loyalist areas said something different.

On the Saturday afternoon it was raining. I walked past the burger vans and a stall blasting out Loyalist music. I asked what was playing. It was 'Echoes of the Somme' sung by

The Platoon. Some of the songs had a surprisingly cheerful tune, at odds with the lyrics about death in some foreign field that is for ever the banks of the Lagan. One burger van had 'Simply the best' on its side. The same slogan was on Johnny Adair's T-shirt.

Mad Dog Adair had turned up at Drumcree earlier in the week with about fifty of the UFF's 2nd Battalion, C Company, all in matching white T-shirts with 'Simply the best' printed on their fronts. But printed below was 'Their only crime – loyalty'. The Red Hand of Ulster had ominously become a red fist on the UFF men's chests. They had been a wonderful spectacle for the world's media.

Now there were just about fifteen sodden men, women and children who were standing beside the charred barricade, peering over a low stone wall and watching some army engineers construct a low green platform, for what purpose nobody seemed to know.

The soldiers were lying on their bellies in the mud, trying to put this thing together in the face of incessant barracking.

'We pay your bloody wages,' one man with a woolly hat shouted down at them. 'Not those boys from the Garvaghy Road. They're all on the fucking dole.'

Another shouted 'What are you making down there, lads? Is it a diving board to dive into that river?'

A few laughed. The river beside the barricade was oily and dirty. A hose led out of it to behind the army and RUC lines. They were saying that this was the water that had been used in the water cannon against the Loyalist protesters.

'You're making a right pig's ear of that wee woman's garden,' another shouted.

There was a constant stream of abuse, which the soldiers did their best to ignore. They looked wet and muddy and fed up. Suddenly a man with a moustache and wearing a green waxed jacket, a pair of binoculars hanging around his neck, started moving through the group, asking excitedly whether anyone had a tow rope. He came back a few minutes later with a blue webbed cord. It was, however, quite short. He looped it over the wall, trying to snare the bright shiny new razor wire on the wet grass. Every time the rope caught the wire the man gave a great tug and the small group all cheered.

It was all quite good-humoured and I felt very relaxed to be there among them. In fact, what had hit me first about this gathering had been the camaraderie. Every single person I passed on the road up to Drumcree Church had said hello. If you were there, you were one of us, the Protestant people under siege.

The man in the waxed jacket now had a second bright idea.

'Is anybody here left-handed?' he shouted excitedly. It wasn't clear why.

An RUC officer in a bulletproof vest and fireproof clothes came round the side of the barricade to see what was going on. He was quite small and this provoked a lot of comment.

'It's Robocop!' shouted somebody from the back. 'The pocket-sized version.'

The RUC man stood there for a few seconds, trying to look relaxed, but then he quickly disappeared again. Everybody cheered.

'You'll be out of a job soon,' somebody shouted. 'The Garda will be doing your job.'

The soldiers worked away regardless, as if we were not there.

A large woman in a bright pink dress leaned over the stone wall and shouted: 'Wait until Johnny comes back and sees all this. He's not going to be well pleased.'

I noticed her later, sitting in her car with her husband and eating an ice cream, with the window down and Loyalist music coming out through the window. Johnny Adair was the new Protestant icon. There would be songs about him soon.

The man beside me was wearing a woolly hat with a loyalist badge on the front. He was pointing at the wire.

'Razor wire is illegal unless it's twelve feet off the ground. This is against the Geneva Convention. That wire is on the ground. What would happen if a child got tangled up in it?'

I shook my head. 'It would be dangerous', I said.

'It would be very dangerous,' he repeated, 'and there are a lot of children around here.' He pointed at a small plumpish boy of about eight or nine wearing a Pokémon sweatshirt who casually walked up to the barricade and chucked a rock over.

'What would happen if that child there fell into the wire?' he asked.

I thought that there was the more immediate question of why the child was allowed to be here in the first place. But I kept it to myself.

In the meantime the young boy had managed to push his head through the gap in the barricade.

'The RUC are putting on their big helmets,' he shouted. 'What does that mean?'

My friend in the woolly hat shook his head mournfully. 'They cleared the hill the other night with a water cannon. It was take no prisoners. I'll tell you, it's going to get worse before it gets better down here.'

He told me that he had been down every day and every night that week for the protest. He was sleeping in a friend's house in Portadown.

'We have to make a stand,' he said, 'or they'll remove all our religious rights and freedoms.'

He told me that he had brought his grandfather to

215

Drumcree last week and his grandfather, he said, had cried when he saw the rows and rows of razor wire.

'He took part in the Normandy landings,' my new friend explained, 'and he told me that he never thought that he'd ever see anything like that again. And especially not here in his own country to prevent him walking down a road in the land he fought for.'

A man in a black Adidas overcoat walked down to the wall with a young girl. He held her up so that she could have a look at the soldiers.

'What are they doing, grandfather?' she asked.

'I'm not sure, love,' he answered.

This man turned out to be a Pastor who ran a mission hall on the Oldpark Road.

'We have to make our stand here,' he told me. He also told me that he had no faith in Tony Blair. 'His allegiances are clear,' he said. 'He claims to belong to the Church of England but he's forever taking Mass. And I've seen his son on television wearing a Republic of Ireland football shirt.' He looked at me knowingly. 'His son supports the Republic of Ireland football team. That should tell you all that you need to know.'

The Pastor had his whole family with him. 'Not because I asked them but because they wanted to be here with me, as a family standing together.'

I had heard Peter Mandelson say that day that the protests had been hijacked by thuggish paramilitaries and that the protesters were nothing more than 'a rabble'. But here was one family who clearly were not.

The Pastor explained his position. 'The Garvaghy residents say that they're offended by the Orangemen but they come out of their houses to be offended. It takes ten minutes for the Orangemen to pass. Ten minutes.'

His friend chipped in – 'And what exactly are they offended by? Is it the Union Flag or the Open Bible? If it's the former then they're fascists because they're trying to stop us displaying our national symbol. If it's the latter, then they're sectarian. Either way we have to stand up to them. Terrorists have turned the state against its law-abiding citizens. That's the crux of the matter.'

It had rained all afternoon and into the evening. I was soaked through like the rest of them – the rest of *us*. As I was preparing to leave I asked the Pastor if he thought that the Orangemen would be allowed to march their traditional route this year.

'I don't think so,' he said.

'And what will happen then?' I asked.

'I don't know,' he replied. 'I just don't know.'

I thanked him and made my way back down the road towards the burger vans.

The Pastor shouted after me, 'But don't give up. Don't forget what Winston Churchill said about the Ulstermen at the Battle of the Somme: "Unquenchable except by death." Tony Blair might need to be reminded of that.'

I knew this quotation and the Pastor had got it a little wrong. The phrase Churchill had actually used was '*Unconquerable* except by death,' and he was not just writing about Ulstermen but about *all* those volunteers, including Ulstermen, who had died at the Somme in the British cause: 'The Flower of that generous manhood which quitted civilian life in every kind of workaday occupation, which came at the call of Britain, and as we may still hope, at the cost of humanity, and came from the most remote parts of her Empire, was shorn away for ever in 1916. Unconquerable except by death, which they had conquered, they have set up a monument of native virtue which will command the wonder, the reverence and the gratitude of our island people as long as we endure as a nation among men.'

But we had lost that generous flower of manhood, either in the field of battle itself or in their mute and debilitating silences in the years after that, where their odd behaviour that was the natural consequence of the battle received little understanding. I felt that what had really happened at the Somme had never been fully articulated: it ate away at the insides of those who had been there and those back home who had sensed the psychological misery of the whole thing and didn't want to probe, like my grandfather George's drinking buddies who never talked about it.

I felt a little trapped right then, claustrophobic, hemmed in on that road in Drumcree, cornered by Martin McGuinness on the radio talking about the last kick of Loyalism, even threatened by the knowledge that had come from my research so far that was starting to give me more understanding of how deep the suffering of my people had really been.

I had come across a new statistic that day but I still needed to check it. According to Fitzpatrick (1989), of the 700 men in the West Belfast Battalion at the Somme, only seventy had survived. And they, in reality, probably didn't have that much to say to anybody, even to their old chums like George Willoughby who knew a thing or two about war of the old-fashioned kind.

21

The next afternoon I found myself back in the park of my childhood, up by my mother's house again. The park was very green. It was also deserted. Branches heavy with leaves bent towards the wet grass like stooped old men. Oak trees, fir trees, three horse chestnut trees, which I found immediately among the others, following some faded map from a childhood memory. Small chestnuts were starting to grow on the trees: years ago I would hit them with short, fat sticks, which were easy to aim and throw, sticks that spun and clattered into the thick branches, releasing the chestnuts that opened when they hit the ground.

The path still wove its way around the outside of the park: I would sometimes run around that path either twelve or sixteen times on a Sunday morning. But the swings had gone and so too had the rocket. We would hang upside down on the rocket, clinging to its tubular metal structure, with wet rust on our fingers, the blood rushing to our heads. Then we'd sit up quickly to feel dizzy.

But there was just the back wall now. Grey and pock-marked and emblazoned with territorial graffiti. Names and nicknames – the same nicknames repeated again and again across the generations: 'Turf', 'Duck', 'Whitesy', 'Hammerhead', as if these monikers were a part of the collective unconscious, to be rediscovered again fifteen or twenty years later. Whitesy, son of Whitesy, the UVF son of a UVF man.

Behind the high wall was a mansion, or there had been twenty or thirty years ago. I wasn't sure how to get to that house without scrambling over the top of the wall, which I wasn't going to do that day. A boy from my school, the Belfast Royal Academy, had lived there years ago. I had never been invited, of course, although we had once banged the door with bricks and scrabbled back over the wall.

The band hut was gone, too. It had been an open shelter from the wind and the rain of North Belfast – the first den before we discovered the little glen at the side of the park. That little glen was a lot tamer than the big glen. The big glen had a river that led to a bleach green, where the linen was bleached, and what we called a 'drop'.

We would line up and then jump one by one from the drop onto the soft ground by the river below. It was one of our tests. We left our indelible deep prints in the soft mud that stayed there for days and reminded us of what we had done. That's what you had to do in our gang. When you were sixteen or seventeen you had to be able to fight.

The big glen was good for weekends of tramping and hiding in the undergrowth, dreaming of being chased by the Sioux or the Cheyenne or the Shawnee. We had daggers in sheaths and bows and quivers for our arrows. In the little glen it was much tamer. We squeezed behind two bars and made a den in the branches.

We brought girls there when we were older, and we would sit around our den in pairs, waiting for one pair to start. Hard lips against yours for three or four minutes at a time so that you had to gulp air from inside her mouth and smell her hot-breath smells. It was like jumping into the deep end of a swimming pool and holding your nose for as long as you could, and when you couldn't any longer you breathed from inside her mouth.

We were experts at finding our way through this thick undergrowth. We knew every step and foothold and when we took girls in there we tried to make it seem convivial and civilized and tame and welcoming for young girls in skirts that we thought were short but probably weren't. We told them that we had a place of our own. And it was our own, in a way. We were quite truthful in that respect. It was our gang's; it belonged to us and nobody touched it.

Two children came into the park on bicycles, a boy of about ten and his younger sister. They were both pretty, pleasant-looking children, with nice, neat clothes. Perhaps they looked a bit like I would have once. Well brought up. They didn't recognize me, of course. I had moved on. I wanted to ask them what their surname was but I was afraid that I wouldn't recognize it. They were cycling around and around on the path. It was just them and me in the park. It was the afternoon of the Twelfth of July and everybody else was elsewhere, in bars or at 'The Field', out celebrating our Protestant heritage.

I had gone that morning to watch the Orangemen march along Royal Avenue. I hadn't watched this procession since I was a boy. I had parked behind St Ann's Cathedral and had made my way towards the sound of the pipes and the flutes and the drums. I felt choked up inside. The swirl of the bagpipes does that to me.

I stopped at the bottom of the Shankill to watch the procession pass. The crowd was two deep on the pavement.

I noticed a couple of children opposite on top of a telephone box, with a Union Jack for a blanket. The lads in the flute bands swaggered along, all pierced ears and eyebrows. Thick gold chains were prominently displayed. One man marched along, shouting down a mobile phone, his voice drowned out by the drums.

A woman with a black perm was dancing up and down just opposite me. She was with a short woman with a round face and a red, white and blue hat and an older woman with a red, white and blue headscarf and no teeth. They all had essentially the same face, albeit across different generations. The women were jigging up and down in time, with the music.

I hadn't seen that dance for years. It was a sort of rocking movement from side to side, cantilevered from the shoulders and from the knees, limbs loose from drink, a vacant smile of pleasant inebriation on their faces.

The woman with the perm stood in front of the spectators, half on the road, facing the bands and the Orangemen. She was asking any passing kiltie to lift their kilt and show her what was underneath. She did this first with a gesture that involved just the fingers curling inwards, almost like tickling a trout, a short fast movement that became more accentuated when nobody responded.

'Come on, love,' she would shout. 'Let's see what you've got under there.'

A large red-haired man in a green tartan lifted the back flap briefly and her friends cheered loudly. I'd almost forgotten that noise. 'Yoooo,' it went, with that long 'oooo' sound. I was trying to laugh, to join in, but I couldn't. I decided to move.

I walked about fifty yards along to a slightly quieter place, and started watching the procession again. And then I noticed him: an elderly grey-haired man – he must have been in his late seventies – marching along, quite straight, with his war medals on display. He was wearing a dark suit, shiny with wear, old shoes, the leather cracked and heavily polished. There was a rolled-up umbrella tucked under his arm, and behind him in a wheelchair came an ancient man with no legs, pushed by a tall thin man who was also very old and who looked hardly capable of pushing the wheelchair even this far. Both wore their Orange sashes. The band in front of them was playing 'Onward Christian Soldiers'.

There was a look of quiet pride and determination on their faces. It was the dignity of the look as much as anything that affected me emotionally. There was something iconic about the image and it has stayed with me ever since. It said something about thrift and hard work and self-reliance, something about strength and resilience. It was the Somme all over again, right in my face, and a memory of a family in the 1960s living in a damp, condemned house in North Belfast, a family who just got on with life without excuses and without any help from anybody else, and a mother who went to Ewart's Mill every day for her children without making a song and dance about it, to make things better. And I was just immensely proud for that moment. I simply felt tremendously privileged to be who I was. Not English, not Scottish, not even Irish.

Just an Ulster Prod.

That afternoon I went back to the park. I had a copy of Thomas Pakenham's *The Boer War* with me because I wanted to find out what my grandfather might have experienced in South Africa in the war declared by the Boers on 11 October 1899, a war that gave the British, in Kipling's words, 'no end of a lesson'.

I had already read a first-hand account by Lieutenant

Neilly about the siege of Mafeking. There is something about sieges that seems particularly pertinent to Ulster Protestants. The Siege of Derry was a defining moment for the Protestants of Ulster, and my mother always said that the Protestants were under siege throughout the Troubles.

The Irish Brigades were led by Major General Hart, who I discovered had the nickname 'General No-Bobs' because apparently he refused to duck his head when shells came flying towards him. According to Pakenham he also deliberately exposed himself to rifle fire as he rode along on his charger.

In February and March 1900 Hart led the Irish battalions at the Tugela River. Hart led them up rock by rock to storm the ridge where the Boers were dug in. They were stranded there for the night with no water or food. The wounded were left to their fate. According to an eye-witness, a Lieutenant Henry Jourdain, 'the shrieks of the wounded during the night were awful'. According to Jourdain the most macabre aspect of the whole night was that the soldiers could hear Dutch hymns drifting across no man's land as the Boers once again celebrated their deliverance.

The next morning the Irish regiments moved down to the valley bottom. The Inniskillings had lost seventy-two per cent of their officers and twenty-seven per cent of their men, the highest proportion of any regiment in the war so far.

'My brave Irish,' said Queen Victoria when she read the war telegrams, but as she read these telegrams the wounded still lay, untended and uncared for, on a hillside by the Tugela River in Natal.

*

I don't know whether George Willoughby was on that hillside by the Tugela River but many Protestants from the mill villages of Belfast would have been there. They were not distinguished from their Catholic neighbours by those in command, all of them just Irish cannon fodder. And what were the defining factors in this war in a land where the elements could kill as many as the enemy, and where the enemy knew the land inside out in a way that their foreign enemies did not?

I suppose that George and his neighbours from Belfast learned a valuable lesson out there in Natal – that fighting for one's home can transform the characters of ordinary men. Men grinning like loafers outside a pub could become something altogether more fierce and more terrible to enable them to stand up to Britain's imperial might. It wouldn't have been lost on the men from the Dublin Fusiliers or the Connaught Rangers either, I am sure.

George signed the Ulster Covenant in 1912 and he joined the UVF to stand up against Home Rule for Ireland. But, of course, he slept in on the day when they landed the guns at Larne. Or he went to bed early because of the drink, one or the other – the story was always changing.

That's the problem with the history of insignificant people: there are a lot of gaps and a lot of guesswork.

In reading about the Boer War, I did learn one small and insignificant bit of information about my own family. My mother always called the sun 'McCormick', or 'Old McCormick', although she never knew where she had got this particular expression from. But this is apparently what the Irish soldiers called their enemy, the sun, during the Boer

War, as fierce an enemy as Old Kroojer himself. George brought that small turn of phrase back with him from the Boer War, as well as perhaps some insight into the importance of standing up and fighting for your home.

I decided that it was time for my run, so I went and got changed in the car. Every Sunday morning when I hadn't felt like running up to the television aerial on Divis or up the Hightown and over Cave Hill, I would do twelve or sixteen laps of this park, just round and round, as if I was in a trance. So that day I started running along those same paths again, always in the same direction, always anticlockwise, towards where the swings used to be.

I noticed that the house opposite the lower gate had every window boarded up. There was paint streaked across the outer walls, broken glass and fragments of rock, and a tin of custard lying on its side in the drive. The tin of custard had obviously been used in the destruction. I realized that this was the house that had been on the front page of the *Irish News*. The photo in the paper had been of a young woman with dark hair and with her back to the camera. She had been wearing a white T-shirt and she was just sitting in the living room of her house amidst the debris of destruction. A Loyalist mob – that was how they had been described – had attacked her house with bricks and rocks and paint because she was living with a Catholic.

This place was still my home but I barely recognized it that day. There was some graffiti on the wall. Sooner or later, it warned, Ligoniel will burn. The melted tarmac neatly marked out the position of each and every barricade that had gone up over the previous days.

*

226

After my sixteen laps, during which I did not see a single soul other than the two children from earlier, I stood with the sweat dripping off me, thinking of how my mother would have reacted.

'It can't be good for you,' she would have said. 'All that sweating.'

I was wondering if she had perhaps heard this from her father who may have come back from the Boer War traumatized by the heat and dust of Natal. I had never thought of that before. I was probably smiling to myself at the thought. Then I noticed that the two children had returned, straddling their bikes, watching me sweating, as if they were a little puzzled why a man on the Twelfth of July should be standing there with the sweat dripping off him.

I called over to them so as not to alarm them. 'All right,' I shouted. 'How's it going?'

'Fine,' the young boy shouted back.

'Good,' I said.

They were still watching me, quite silent.

'I've just been training,' I said. 'For marathons.'

'Oh,' the boy's sister said.

I smiled at them and this time they smiled back.

'Are you English, mister?' the boy shouted, as if that might explain my strange behaviour.

'No,' I said. But I did not elaborate. I went and sat on the grass and they played, running around in circles out in front of me as if they didn't want to approach this strange creature too closely. But they were smiling at me more and more, so I knew that they felt quite safe.

I asked the boy on the bicycle if he'd seen what had happened with the paint and the stones and I pointed over at the house outside the front gate.

'It happened at night, mister,' he said. 'I could hear it all, the shouting and all that, but I wasn't allowed out to see what was going on. My mother and father won't let me out when there's trouble like that going on.'

He was almost apologetic that he couldn't help me.

'What was it all about?' I asked, wiping the sweat off my forehead with the palm of my hand.

'It was a mob that attacked that house,' he replied as his sister looked on, holding the handlebars of her red bicycle.

'Why that particular house?' I asked.

'I don't know,' he said. 'I think that they were after somebody.'

'Somebody in particular?' I enquired.

'Oh yes, it was somebody that they were already after,' he said.

'Was he a Fenian?' I suggested. I was pushing him now and loading the question to see how he would respond to one of his own.

'It was definitely a Catholic they were after,' he said. 'But I'm also pretty sure that it was somebody in particular that they were after. It was definitely somebody they were already looking for.'

'Not just a random Catholic, then?' I was thinking of the question that I had asked Hacksaw for my television documentary, to discover if *any* Catholic would have qualified to be a potential victim in this context.

'Oh, no,' he said. 'They wouldn't just do that.'

I smiled knowingly at his innocence, or it could have been at my own. His sister called over to him that she wanted to go and play. It was boring just standing there, she said.

'I'm sorry,' the boy said politely. 'I'll have to go.'

'Okay,' I said and I threw him a smile. 'I'll see you around.'

They cycled off, the boy looking back over his shoulder at me two or three times. I walked back down to the front gate of the park and glanced over at the house with the paint on the wall and then at my mother's opposite.

I had been touched by the boy's innocence and by the fact that he knew right from wrong, that he wasn't going to be confused with my weasel words like 'Fenian', and that he was being brought up all right in the midst of this chaos. It was almost as if I had been shocked to catch a glimpse of the ordinary decent people in this area, the respectable hard-working families who formed the vast majority of the people who lived around here, despite all that they had been put through for thirty years.

The cowboys, as my mother called them, with their rocks and their paint and their big tins of custard, got all the attention, even from a so-called experienced observer like myself. I suppose that this well-turned-out boy, with his shy, quiet smile and his eager-to-please manner, reminded me of myself. Just some child whom you've never met before who speaks like you might have once talked, who doesn't really understand sectarianism because that's not how he's been brought up, whose mother keeps him neat and tidy and makes sure that he does his homework, who may have an uncle somewhere who himself is a big fucking Taig.

I dried my sweat and got back into my car, pale from my run but happier than I had been for many months. Meeting this boy had cheered me up.

Later I contacted the Regimental Museum of the Royal Inniskilling Fusiliers to find out more about my grandfather's personal involvement in the Boer War. They provided me with details of the movements and engagements of the Second Battalion of the regiment, which I knew my grandfather had been in. The First Battalion had fought at Colenso; the Second Battalion apparently had not. They did not arrive in South Africa until 7 February 1902. The Second Battalion acted as emergency troops 'ready at a moment's notice to reinforce a threatened part of the line'. Their official history warns me that: 'To follow the fortunes of a regiment in ordinary warfare is comparatively easy, but to keep in touch with the movements of the individual companies of the "special services battalion" in the spring of 1902 on the veld of South Africa is almost impossible.'

However, a contingent of them did, under Colonel Colenbrander, fight against Boer commandos commanded by General Beyers at Pyl Kop, a tract of wild, broken and mountainous country near Pietersburg, about one hundred and fifty miles north of Johannesburg. A Lieutenant Colonel Murray, who was wounded in the abdomen, wrote: 'The men behaved splendidly . . . Colenbrander is enthusiastic about the Regiment, its pluck and endurance. Some companies have been for two days without food or water or shelter and you never hear a complaint from a man. Indeed, it is impossible to beat the Irish soldier in my opinion. Lord Kitchener has telegraphed his congratulations to the troops engaged. Up to date we have taken or killed 120 Boers, 1,000 head of cattle and 26 wagons.'

According to Colenbrander's report of the attack, four officers of the Inniskillings were hit, whereas the other ranks suffered hardly at all. The official history of the regiment points out by way of explanation that: 'It must be remembered that there was plenty of cover for the men on the rocky hills, but in leading their companies the officers had to expose themselves greatly.'

My grandfather George probably took no chances.

22

I may have discovered that my father's family had come from the Dromore area, but I had still not found anything tangible apart from that one small entry for Sam Beatty from Drumaknockan in *Griffith's Primary Valuation*, which told me that at least one of my ancestors had owned some land in Ulster. But armed with a copy of *Gravestone Inscriptions*, Volume 19, County Down, I returned to Dromore. This book told me that there was a headstone to 'Beatty' in the graveyard of Dromore Cathedral. 'Erected by James Beatty, U.S.A. 1899, in loving remembrance of his father James Beatty of Dromore who departed this life in 1829. Also of his mother Mary Beatty who departed this life in 1878. And of his sisters Sarah Margaret and Sarah who died in infancy.'

The book also informed me that the white marble headstone was broken in two.

The graveyard of Dromore Cathedral is on the banks of a reedy river, with clumps of weeds in the middle and lapping water and high grasses at the edges. I thought it was a peaceful place. I found a John Gill of Drumaknockan, buried there in 1752, which reminded me that Protestants had been in this area for some time.

However, the only Beattie in this cemetery was buried in a small nondescript grave with no details on any headstone, which disappointed me greatly. Until recently my father lying in Roselawn had had no headstone because we hadn't been able to afford one when he'd died in the 1960s. But in the last few years we had got him one and my brother's name had been added, and now my mother's, so that our family history will be that much clearer for those who come after me. I knew that my father's people were from around Dromore but there seemed to be no real trace of Sam or any of his descendants. I tried all the graveyards in the city with no success.

I had, however, bought a copy of the *Ordnance Survey Memoirs* of Ireland for the Mid-Down area. In 1824 a House of Commons committee had recommended a townland survey of Ireland to facilitate a valuation for local taxation. The Duke of Wellington, who was then Prime Minister, had authorized this, the first Ordnance Survey of Ireland. As well as the sketching, drawing and engraving of maps, memoirs were written to accompany them. These memoirs cover such things as the natural features of the landscape, the topography, and aspects of the social economy including descriptions of the schools and the religion and the habits of the people.

What was life like for the Beatties in Drumaknockan or thereabouts in the 1830s? According to Lieutenant G. A. Bennett, writing on 29 October 1834, Dromore itself 'is said to be derived from the word drum, "a back", and more, "great", or "the great back of a hill", which would answer the situation of the town. It is situated in the western part of the county of Down and barony of Lower Iveagh and diocese of Dromore, and is bounded on the north by the parishes of Moira and Hillsborough, on the east by Annahilt, on the south-east by Dromara, on the west by Donaghcloney and Magheralin.'

Drumaknockan is mentioned specifically in his account because it is the site of the largest bog in the parish. In terms of topography Dromore contains the cathedral, which is described as 'a poor building'. The people of Dromore were of many denominations, both Protestant and Catholic, the memoir says, and Bennett notes that: 'Neither do the habits of the people differ. The food and fuel are the same and there is no peculiarity of costume.'

Later on Bennett writes that: 'The streets are narrow, dirty and the outskirts hilly. In the whole town there are 261 houses of 1, 148 of 2 and 47 of 3-storeys. Of these 215 are thatched and the remainder are slated. Those of 1-storey are situated on the outskirts and are perhaps as wretched-looking hovels as are to be met with in the north of Ireland . . . At present the town is neither lighted, paved or watched . . . There are no libraries or reading rooms. There was formerly a book club but, the members dying away, the books were sold. There are no banks. An attempt was made about 12 years since to establish a savings bank but it did not succeed.'

In Dromara, which is even closer to Drumaknockan, the conditions were similar. 'In general, the houses are stone and thatched, with 2 or 3 rooms and a kitchen on the ground floor, but in the mountainous part they are commonly built with sods or loose stones and have a most wretched appearance.' In Dromara there was little weaving and the chief employment was agriculture. The majority who lived in the Dromara townland were Roman Catholic. The history of the Dromara parish was that: 'The parish forms part of the lands granted by patent of Queen Elizabeth to Ever MacRory Maguinness, which were forfeited in the war of 1641 and afterwards granted by Charles II to Colonel Hill.' This gave me some inkling of Sam Beatty's life in Drumaknockan, working the peaty land of a bog, with his Catholic neighbours helping him to cultivate the land. It was my first link back to the Plantations of Ulster, which had always been such an abstract and impersonal idea.

I enjoyed these memoirs partly because they were not the words of professional historians but rather the accounts of first-hand observers, more like direct reportage than history. It gave me some connection with the past and perhaps a different impression of the Ulster Plantations, lands granted to some Protestants but on which Protestants and Catholics worked side by side. Bennett's words – 'Neither do the habits of the people differ' – rang in my ears.

But there was nothing to see in Dromore so I set out to find Drumaknockan once more, to try to capture some emotional response from the land itself.

And then something quite peculiar happened.

There were no signs to Drumaknockan – I remembered that solitary road sign on my previous visit – and I took a wrong turning on those quiet country lanes and got completely and utterly lost. I drove for miles in tranquil countryside with no passers-by to ask for directions. I eventually ended up in Donaghcloney, which reminded me a little bit of North Belfast with its greyish, dull-looking houses and kerbstones painted red, white and blue, and its Union Jacks and Red Hand of Ulster flags fluttering from the poles in front of the houses. It felt curiously familiar.

On the left-hand side of the road was a churchyard so I

stopped and went to have a look. And there in the corner of the churchyard under a rookery were as many headstones with the name 'Beattie' on them as I could ever have wished for: Robert Beattie, Thomas Beattie, Edward Beattie – who'd died on active service in the First World War – Samuel Beattie, William Beattie and Maxwell Beattie. I had spent many years scanning war memorials and gravestones in different parts of the British Isles for a trace of my past, and suddenly it seemed that here they all were, gathered together in one small place.

Just up from Maxwell Beattie lay Private Bernard McQuirt who had won his regiment's first Victoria Cross at Rowa India on 6 January 1858. It reminded me again of George Willoughby and his service in India. McQuirt, I thought, was an odd surname for an Ulster Protestant, but on reading Doherty and Truesdale's *Irish Winners of the Victoria Cross*, I discovered that 'McQuirt' was illiterate, which explained why his name was spelt so oddly. His real name was the more Ulster-sounding McCourt. He had fought in the 95th Derbyshire Regiment in Rewa India (incorrectly spelt as 'Rowa') and had taken part in close-quarter fighting in the town, sustaining five sabre cuts and a bullet wound. Apparently, Queen Victoria could not bear to look at him when she presented him with his medal.

My grandfather George Willoughby did not serve in India during McCourt's time. He was there later, at the turn of the century, in the Khyber Pass as part of the Peshawar Column, Tirah Expeditionary Force, under the command of Brigadier General A. G. Hammond. The official history of the Inniskillings tells me that: 'Khyber Zakha Khel had made no sign of submission. Brigadier General Hammond took active measures to punish them for their behaviour in closing the Khyber against all traffic, in cutting up a garrison of native troops and in destroying the British forts in the pass. Day after day he destroyed their villages, blew up their towers, *looted* the forage they had collected for the winter.'

I suppose that this is more the reality of war than individual derring-do, and perhaps it was all this to which George was 'indifferent'.

This chance find of the graveyard in Donaghcloney would have been more satisfactory if my people had actually come from here rather than from Drumaknockan. The Beatties in Donaghcloney would have been connected with the linen industry. Bennett's memoirs of Donaghcloney told me that this townland had an extensive bleach green and that: 'The houses have a neat and clean appearance.' This made me laugh because I thought about my mother washing the step out on the street, the way that women did in the Belfast of the 1960s, polishing the pavement in a neat semicircle.

I also discovered that in Donaghcloney in the 1830s: 'The people have no amusements except dancing' and that: 'There are no scientific or literary institutions, libraries or reading rooms but the inhabitants club together and take in newspapers: the *Belfast Standard* or *Farmer's Journal* is the present favourite.'

There were a lot of Beatties there, but it was the wrong branch of the family, or so I thought. When I got back to Belfast I was told quite by chance about the Ulster Historical Foundation and I asked them to provide me, from their computerized church records, with details of my family tree at least back to Sam Beatty, the landowner from Drumaknockan in the 1830s.

It only took the researcher a few minutes to answer my request. I was surprised that it was so easy, having always believed that this search would be much more difficult and that your personal history was not at the mercy of a push of a cold computer button. His words came as something of a shock to me.

'Your grandfather Sam Beattie, who was a motor mechanic,' he said, 'got married on 18 September 1897, aged twenty-five. His father was also called Sam. He was a labourer or sometimes a weaver. Your great-grandfather Sam got married on 9 June 1859. His age isn't on the marriage certificate but he must have been born in the 1830s. But his father wasn't Sam Beatty, the 1830s landowner from Drumaknockan, but a Maxwell Beatty, who was a labourer. They lived in the Quilly and Donaghcloney area.'

The researcher helpfully printed out the result of his searches, a neat pile of A4 pages that summarized my family history. It took a few minutes on a computer to generate this information and there in front of me lay the long list of the occupations of the generations that had gone before me, a list that might help to explain who and what I am.

It turns out that I come from a long line of labourers, who sometimes, it seems, found work in the weaving industry. And on my mother's side the picture is very similar: the Willoughbys and the Nochers tended to be labourers as well, again often working in the linen industry. There were no big landowners hidden back there, and no Dunville connections that were anywhere apparent that day. Nothing was in that pile of A4 sheets, I suppose, except the mundane history of the Ulster province, and hints of the hard work that had made Ulster what it was.

I also smiled at the image of this dour little village called Donaghcloney with its flags and its bunting hanging out there limp and tattered in the July wind, and the thought that I had at last found some place in Ulster that was indisputably part of me. There were no real surprises in the past.

I rang the minister of the local church, St Patrick's, for a chat one evening, and told him about my research and he informed me that one of his churchwardens was a John Beattie. The minister told me that John was a very quiet man, and that he would need to warn him that I wished to interview him.

John turned out to be a retired electrician, a quietly spoken man. My brother had served his time as an electrician before he'd packed it all in to climb mountains and to seek adventure on the Goddess of Joy. I mentioned my brother's former occupation to John without elaborating further.

'It just shows you, doesn't it?' John Beattie said, and we left it at that.

I have never returned to Donaghcloney, but I had an image of this quiet little Ulster backwater fixed in my mind – until, that is, I read McKittrick, Kelter, Feeney and Thornton's extraordinary book *Lost Lives*, which documents in encyclopaedic and objective detail all the lives lost in the present Troubles. From this book, I discovered that Robin Jackson, known as 'The Jackal', who is considered to have been the most active Loyalist killer of the Troubles, personally responsible for fifty or so deaths, lived in Donaghcloney and died of cancer at his home there in 1998. I also learned that in 1989 Patrick Feeney from Tyrone was murdered by the UFF while manning a security gate at the Ewart Liddell linen mill in Donaghcloney. Even a Ewart's linen mill had come back into my life.

It was no wonder then, I thought to myself, that

Donaghcloney seemed so familiar to a man born and reared at the turn-of-the-road in North Belfast.

At the end of my visit, I went back to the turn-of-the-road just to reflect. There was some new graffiti that day on the gable wall just opposite my mother's old house. It read 'GODISNOWHERE.'

I thought about the Troubles and what my mates had done and what had happened to my neighbours and friends. I thought that it sometimes seemed that God was indeed nowhere during some of the most terrible years of the conflict. But below the graffiti somebody had scrawled something else. I had to go over to the gable wall to make it out. It said 'Now read this again.' So I did, and I parsed the phrase above differently this second time. It read: 'GOD IS NOW HERE.' I wrote this down and thought of my mother. It was a brilliantly clear image – she was happy and she was smiling, and I smiled back, by way of reciprocation. I could hear her speaking and there was no sense of sarcasm or anger in her voice.

'You're some pup,' she said.

She didn't have any of her cares in this image. And I didn't try to put the imaginal memory into words until now. I didn't try to explain it, I just enjoyed it, and stored it away. It was a clearer smile than any photograph, and hopefully more permanent than any photograph that fades in a damp mill house.

There had only ever been one tangible thread linking me with my past and that had been my mother. She was that thread and part of my motivation was to find out the truth about the Dunville story and our family background. After all, I was the one who had been given all the chances in life.

I was the one who could do the research and write it all down in a permanent way that doesn't fade as memory does. And I did find some sense of identity by attempting to reach back into my memories and by following old routes back through my childhood to reach for my Ulster Protestant heritage and by discovering that I may not have been a Dunville but I was certainly a Willoughby and probably a Beattie too. I learned about the Somme and the immense courage of my people on the battlefield and the suffering that followed them home to those same little mill houses with the damp walls where nothing was said. And their mothers would have put up with it all.

I can see their faces now.

Recently I have started noticing things about myself. When my daughter Zoë doesn't ring me, I ask her why she doesn't ring me more often and why she doesn't have the time to visit me and I ask her what she actually does all day apart from going out and enjoying herself. I have started leaving numbers calculated and written down in pencil on scraps of paper, like my mother did, just checking that I get what I am owed. And I sometimes sit up at nights wondering if there was more to the Dunville story than I have so far managed to uncover and regret that I wasn't the kind of academic with the investigative skills that would allow me to research history properly.

Last year I had an illness that made my left ankle swell; it was my first visit to the doctor since I was a child. It was so ironic that this illness should attack my ankle of all places; it was like a salutary lesson for me, or a message. It stopped me running for a few months, so I found myself crawling around the gym on my hands and knees to climb onto the equipment to work my upper body.

For four months I was on crutches. I was bad-tempered and impatient, and I slept in the bedroom that my mother used to stay in when she came to England. It still smelt of her and I would sit up in bed, just like her, reading and with a dressing gown over my shoulders. Sometimes at night I would catch a glimpse of myself in the mirror and in that momentary reflection see exactly what connects me to my past, without having to travel anywhere.

And perhaps in these moments – in this darkened room lit by a single lamp over by the bed, with such a familiar and evocative sour-smelling scent on the duvet and on the sheets – I also glimpsed my own future.

Core material used in the text

Armitage, S. and Crawford, R. (Eds.) (1998) *The Penguin Book of Poetry from Britain and Ireland since 1945.* Viking: London.

Armstrong-Jones, R. (1917) 'The psychopathy of the barbed wire.' *Nature,* 100, 1–3.

Armstrong-Jones, R. (1917) 'Shell-shock and its lessons – a reply.' *Nature,* 100, 66.

Barker, Pat (1992) *Regeneration.* Penguin Books: London.

Bardon, Jonathan. (1992) A History of Ulster. Blackstaff Press: Belfast.

Bartlett, F. (1932) *Remembering: A Study in Experimental and Social Psychology.* Cambridge University Press: London.

Beattie, G. (1986) *Survivors of Steel City: A Portrait of Sheffield.* Chatto & Windus: London.

Beattie, G. (1992) *We Are The People: Journeys through the Heart of Protestant Ulster.* Heinemann: London.

Beattie, G. (1998) *The Corner Boys.* Victor Gollancz: London.

Beattie, G. and Doherty, K. (1995) '"I saw what really happened": the discursive construction of victims and perpetrators in firsthand accounts of paramilitary violence in Northern Ireland.' *Journal of Language and Social Psychology,* 14, 408–433.

Black, G.F. (1965) *The Surnames of Scotland: Their Origin, Meaning, and History.* New York Public Library: New York.

Blackburn, R. (1965) 'Emotionality, repression-sensitization, and maladjustment.' *British Journal of Psychiatry,* 111, 399–400.

243

Churchill, W. S. (1900) *London to Ladysmith via Pretoria*. Longmans Green: London.

Churchill, W. S. (1927) *The World Crisis 1916–1918*: Part 1. Thornton Butterworth: London.

Day, A. and McWilliams, P. (eds.). (1992) *Ordnance Survey Memoirs of Ireland: Parishes of County Down III 1833–8*. The Institute of Irish Studies: The Queen's University of Belfast.

Doherty, R. and Truesdale, D. (2000) *Irish Winners of the Victoria Cross*. Four Courts Press: Dublin.

Fitzpatrick, R. (1989) *God's Frontiersmen: The Scots-Irish Epic*. Weidenfeld and Nicolson: London.

Gleitman, H., Fridlund, A. J. and Reisberg, D. (1999) *Psychology (5th edition)*. Norton: New York.

Hart-Davis, R. (ed.) (1983) *The War Poems of Siegfried Sassoon*. Faber and Faber: London.

Kissen, D.M. (1966) 'The significance of personality in lung cancer in men.' *Annals of the New York Academy of Science*, 125, 820–826.

Lee, V. and Beattie, G. (1998) 'The rhetorical organization of verbal and nonverbal behaviour in emotion talk.' *Semiotica*, 120, 39–92.

Lee, V. and Beattie, G. (2000) 'Why talking about negative emotional experiences is good for your health: a microanalytic perspective.' *Semiotica*, 130, 1–81.

Leed, E. J. (1979) *No Man's Land: Combat and Identity in World War I*. Cambridge University Press: Cambridge.

MacDonagh, M. (1917) *The Irish on the Somme*. Hodder and Stoughton: London.

Macdonald, L. (1988) *1914–1918: Voices and Images of the Great War*. Penguin: London.

McClelland, D.C. (1979) 'Inhibited power motivation and high blood pressure in men.' *Journal of Abnormal Psychology*, 88, 182–190.

McGuinness, F. (1986) *Observe the Sons of Ulster Marching Towards the Somme*. Faber and Faber: London.

McKay, S. (2000) *Northern Protestants: An Unsettled People*. The Blackstaff Press: Belfast.

McKittrick, D., Kelters, S., Feeney, B. and Thornton, C. (1999) *Lost Lives: the Stories of the Men, Women and Children who died as a Result of the Northern Ireland Troubles*. Mainstream Publishing: London.

Milgram, S. (1974) *Obedience to Authority: An Experimental View*. Harper & Row: New York.

Miller, E. (ed.) (1942) *The Neurosis in War*. New York.

Mott, F.W. (1919) *War Neurosis and Shell-Shock*. Hodder and Stoughton: London.

Moynahan, B. (1997) *The British Century: a Photographic History of the Last Hundred Years*. Random House: New York.

O'Hart, J. (1892) *Irish Pedigrees, or the Origin and Stem of the Irish Nation*. Genealogical Publishing Co.: Dublin.

Orr, P. (1987) *The Road to the Somme: Men of the Ulster Division Tell Their Story*. Blackstaff Press: Belfast.

Owen, W. (1917) Dulce et Decorum est. Reprinted in Walter, G. (ed.) (1997) *Rupert Brooke & Wilfred Owen: Collected Poems*. Everyman: London.

Pakenham, T. (1979) *The Boer War*. Abacus: London.

Pear, T.H. (1918) 'The war and psychology.' *Nature*, 102, 88–89.

Pear, T.H. and Smith, G. E. (1917) Shell-shock and its lessons. *Nature*, 100, 64–66.

Pennebaker, J.W. (1995) 'Emotion, disclosure, and health: an overview.' In Pennebaker, J.W. (Ed.) *Emotion, Disclosure and Health*. American Psychological Association: Washington.

Pennebaker, J.W. (1997) 'Writing about emotional experiences as a therapeutic process.' *Psychological Science*, 8, 162–166.

Pennebaker, J.W. and Beall, S. (1986) 'Confronting a traumatic event: toward an understanding of inhibition and disease.' *Journal of Abnormal Psychology*, 95, 274–281.

Richards, W. (1888) *Her Majesty's Army: A Descriptive Account of the Various Regiments Now Comprising the Queen's Forces, from their First Establishment to the Present Time*. Virtue & Co.: London.

Rivers, W.H.R. (1918) 'The repression of war experience.' *The Lancet*, Feb. 2, 173–177.

Rolston, B. (1992) *Drawing Support: Murals in the North of Ireland*. Beyond the Pale Publications: Belfast.

Rolston, B. (1995) Drawing Support 2: *Murals of War and Peace*. Beyond the Pale Publications: Belfast.

Royal Inniskilling Fusiliers Official History: From December 1688 to July 1914. (1928) Constable: London.

Showalter, E. (1987) *The Female Malady: Women, Madness and English Culture*, 1830–1980. Virago: London.

245

Simmel, E. (1921) *Psychoanalysis and the War Neuroses*. London.

Walker, J. M. S. (1916) 'The Somme: 21st Casualty Clearing Station, 1–3 July.' In Moynihan, M. (ed.) (1973) *People at War 1914–1918*. David & Charles: London.

Yealland, L. (1918) *Hysterical Disorders of Warfare*. Macmillan and Co.: London.

Acknowledgements

Sara Holloway and Bella Shand were amazing and provided extremely valuable comments on drafts of this book. Robert Kirby from Peters Fraser and Dunlop was my agent and believed in the project from the start. *The Guardian* first published the pieces on my eleven-plus and Isaac the barber, *The Irish Times* the piece on my uncle's death and the *New Statesman* the piece on Drumcree. I thank them for their interest.